Rational Man

Henry Babcock Veatch

Rational Man

A Modern Interpretation
of Aristotelian Ethics

Henry B. Veatch

Preface and Annotated Bibliography
by Douglas B. Rasmussen

amagi

Liberty Fund
Indianapolis

Amagi books are published by Liberty Fund, Inc.,
a foundation established to encourage study of the
ideal of a society of free and responsible individuals.

The cuneiform inscription that appears in the logo and
serves as a design element in all Liberty Fund books
is the earliest-known written appearance of the word
"freedom" (*amagi*), or "liberty." It is taken from a clay
document written about 2300 B.C. in the Sumerian
city-state of Lagash.

Printed in the United States of America
07   06   05   04   03   P   5   4   3   2   1

Library of Congress Cataloging-in-Publication Data
Veatch, Henry Babcock.
    Rational man: a modern interpretation of Aristotelian ethics /
Henry B. Veatch; preface by Douglas B. Rasmussen.
        p.   cm.
    Originally published: Bloomington: Indiana University Press, 1962.
    With new pref. and annotated bibliography.
    Includes bibliographical references (p.   ) and index.
ISBN 0-86597-393-8 (pbk.: alk. paper)
1. Ethics.   2. Aristotle.   I. Title.
BJ37 .V43   2003
171'.3—dc21   2002029651

LIBERTY FUND, INC.
8335 Allison Pointe Trail, Suite 300, Indianapolis, Indiana 46250-1684

To J. S. V. *and* E. W. F. V.

in the hope that some day

"they should see with their eyes

and hear with their ears

and should understand with their hearts"

Contents

Preface

Rational Man, which first appeared in 1962, brings Aristotelian ethics alive to the contemporary reader. Its author, Henry Babcock Veatch, was a leading neo-Aristotelian of the twentieth century. Born in Evansville, Indiana, in 1911, Veatch was educated at Harvard University, from which he received his doctorate in 1936. His mentor at Harvard was John Wild, and he was influenced by the twentieth-century neo-Thomists Jacques Maritain and Etienne Gilson. Veatch taught for twenty-eight years at Indiana University, for eight years at Northwestern University, and for more than ten years at Georgetown University. Veatch was a prolific writer, an outstanding teacher, a skillful debater, and, above all, a perceptive philosopher. At different times, he served as president of both the American Philosophical Association (Western Division) and the American Catholic Philosophical Association. To those who knew him, Veatch was a man of energy, good humor, and graciousness. Most of all he was a gentleman. He retired in 1983 but was active philosophically throughout his retirement years. He died in 1999. A Festschrift* appeared at the time of his retirement from Georgetown University.

Veatch was an Aristotelian through and through, but anyone familiar with his work would see immediately that he was conversant with the latest contemporary issues in philosophy. Veatch was well known for championing his Aristotelianism against contemporary philosophical fashions. Indeed, *Rational Man* is but one of a series of works in which Veatch challenged many of the prevailing beliefs of his time, especially those of Anglo-American philosophy. Those interested in Veatch's other major books and articles may wish to consult the anno-

---

*Rocco Porreco, ed., *The Georgetown Symposium on Ethics: Essays in Honor of Henry Babcock Veatch* (Lanham, Md.: University Press of America, 1984).

tated bibliography that follows this preface. These works reveal a thinker with an eye for what is crucial philosophically and a philosopher who was concerned with the truth of things—not the latest intellectual styles.

Rational Man is, however, the most distinctive of all of Veatch's works; it accomplishes what is nearly impossible to achieve. It engages both the expert and the beginner. Both can read and profit from this work. There is substantial scholarship and philosophical sophistication in these pages, but the work is never dry or heavy-handed. Veatch's philosophical learning does not get in the way of the message. The arguments are crisp; the reading is lively; and the examples are numerous, particularly those from literature.

Veatch's arguments in *Rational Man* were not only in conflict with several dominant philosophical views of his time, but they also remain in conflict with many of those today. His arguments sought to establish three claims: (1) that ethical knowledge is possible; (2) that ethical knowledge is grounded in human nature; and (3) that the purpose of ethics is to show the individual human being how to "self-perfect," which was Veatch's way of writing about *eudaimonia* in Aristotelian moral theory. Moreover, these moral claims were defended without appeal to religious revelation but "solely on what used to be known as the natural light of reason." Veatch was an advocate of what is commonly called "natural law" moral theory; such a theory was for Veatch, however, not to be confused with what is today called "divine command theory." Accordingly, ethics is based on the requirements for human moral development—what Veatch and others call "self-perfection"—and never merely on what is commanded by a deity. This does not mean, however, that ethics and religion were necessarily incompatible for Veatch; rather, it means only that *Rational Man* is simply a book on "ethics without religion."

Veatch's use of the words "self-perfection," "perfection," and "perfect" may not be familiar to contemporary readers. "Perfect" comes from the Latin *perfectus* and its Greek counterpart *teleios*. *Perfectus* implies that a thing is completed or finished; this involves the idea of a thing's having a nature that is its end (*telos*) or function (*ergon*). Thus, it should be clear that, when Veatch spoke of how to "perfect" oneself, he did not mean that one should become Godlike, immune to degeneration, or incapable of harm. Rather, it is to fulfill those potentialities and capacities that makes one fully human.

Veatch's understanding of natural law should be situated. Perhaps the best way to do this is to consider one of Veatch's favorite citations, which is found in the writing of the Elizabethan divine Richard Hooker. Hooker's characterization of law in general is found in his classic work, *Of the Laws of Ecclesiastical Polity.*

> That which doth assign unto each thing the kind, that which doth moderate the force and power, that which doth appoint the form and measure of working, the same we term *a Law.*

For Veatch, the concept of "natural law" is based on the idea that a thing's nature is not only that in virtue of which a thing acts or behaves the way it does, but it is also the standard or measure in terms of which we judge whether the thing's action or behavior is all that it might or could have been. It is the standard in terms of which we judge whether it is functioning well or appropriately. In other words, not only do we think that things, especially human beings, have a nature that governs how they act or behave but that the fulfillment or perfection of their nature is their end or function.

We commonly think of human artifacts as having a proper function. For example, the proper function of a knife is to cut. To claim that an entity has a *natural* function, however, is to claim that an entity has a proper function because of what it is, not because of its being designed by someone for a certain activity. In this case, "proper" means "essential to the entity." An entity that fulfills its proper function is an entity that functions well or excellently—indeed, as the ancient Greeks would say, with *arête,* which was their term for "virtue." The claim that an entity has a natural function, however, does not stop here. It rests on the further claim that an entity has an end in view of what it is. Thus, the natural function of a thing is determined because of its natural end. In this context, "end" means "that-for-the-sake-of-which"; it does not necessarily mean "conscious purpose." Natural law ethics is for Veatch ultimately a natural-end ethics.

Many members of the modern intellectual community hold that believing in natural ends or functions is beyond the philosophical, as well as the scientific, pale. Teleology is out of date in this scientific day and age. Veatch argued, however, that one cannot infer that there are absolutely no natural ends simply because contemporary scientific methodology does not have a place for them. Further, he argued that natural ends are not easily eliminated. Throughout *Rational Man*, Veatch suggests that natural ends are part of our ordinary, common-sense understanding of the process of change. In addition, later in his career Veatch came to believe that the new developments in contemporary biological and evolutionary theory pointed to the idea that living things possess an irreducible potential for their mature state that cannot be explained simply by appealing to chemistry and physics. Reductionism was, for him, theoretically unsound. In other words, contemporary biology supports the idea of natural functions or ends for living things; evolutionary theory, therefore, need be seen in conflict only with an *anthropomorphic* conception of teleology.

Regardless of how natural teleology might be defended, Veatch held that there are natural ends. There are at least some ways of being that are inherently valuable or good—specifically, those that constitute the perfection of a living thing's nature—and when such ways of being are actualized through choice, they are choice-worthy and the basis for ethics. In the language of his day, Veatch held that not all facts are value free. He argued in the chapter "But What If God Is Dead" of *Rational Man* that goodness is, *pace* G. E. Moore, "definable." According to Veatch, we can say what goodness is for a human being, and we can do this by understanding our natural end. Attaining our natural end is our ultimate good. Veatch thus challenged the very concept of the so-called naturalistic fallacy, which was (and is) the very core or paradigm of what often has been called "analytic" ethics. Veatch's later work, *For an Ontology of Morals*, explored these matters in even greater detail.

The central issue in *Rational Man* is, nonetheless, the claim that our nature as human beings can provide us with guidance regarding how we should conduct our lives. Veatch's approach to this issue certainly belongs to the natural law ethical tradition; throughout his writings, he opposed both a desire- and a duty-based ethics. His approach is also markedly different in some respects from the natural law tradition or, at least, from how that tradition is often perceived. The most direct way to appreciate those differences and so locate Veatch in the natural law tradition is to consider what he had to say about the following questions: What is our human good? and How do we go about attaining it?

Veatch's answer to these questions relied on Aristotle. Our good is what Aristotle called *eudaimonia*. Though the traditional English translation of this term is "happiness," Veatch often simply called it "living rationally or intelligently." Later in his career, he adopted the term "human flourishing." For Veatch, the human good is never merely doing whatever one wants. Yet, Veatch's answer also differed from Aristotle's. Veatch took issue with Aristotle's claim, found in chapters seven and eight of Book X of the *Nicomachean Ethics,* that the human good consists precisely in a life of contemplation (*theoria*)—that is, in the pursuit of knowledge for knowledge's sake. Instead, Veatch chose to follow Aristotle's claim of Book I of the *Ethics.* Our human good is "the practical life of man possessing reason." It consists in our living in accordance with a "rational principle," and "rational principle," in turn, is to be understood broadly as intelligence: intelligence that may be applied to art, craft, science, philosophy, politics, or any area of human endeavor. Such living includes capacities possessed by other animals, such as those for pleasure and health and many other things as well. Our distinguishing characteristic, our capacity to reason and choose, characterizes the *modality* through which the development of these other faculties will be successful.

Veatch's reason for diverging from Aristotle is significant and revealing.

> The basis for our disagreement is simply our unshakeable conviction that living is not for the sake of knowing, but rather that it is toward intelligent living that all our powers and capacities are ultimately directed, including our powers of knowledge, and that it is the man himself who counts more than all his knowledge, no matter how great the latter may be.

Basic goods, like knowledge, are for the sake of the fulfillment of individual human beings; individuals are not for the sake of achieving basic goods. It is the perfection of the individual human being, not disembodied reasoning, that matters ultimately. Our true end or good consists, Veatch emphasized, "in *living* intelligently."

Accordingly, human flourishing is not, for Veatch, a single "dominant" activity that reduces all other activities to mere instrumental
value. Instead, it is a way of living that is an "inclusive" activity. It en-
compasses such basic goods as knowledge, health, friendship, creativ-
ity, beauty, and pleasure. Attaining those goods is both productive and
expressive of human flourishing. They are thus valuable not as mere
means to human flourishing but as partial realizations of that flourishing. The entire process requires the intellectual virtue of practical wisdom—what Aristotle called *phronēsis*—and the development of rational moral dispositions, or moral virtues.

Practical wisdom is *the* intellectual virtue for Veatch. It is never
merely cleverness or means-end reasoning. Rather, it is the ability of
the individual at the time of action to discern in particular and contingent circumstances what is required morally. Practical wisdom is the
intelligent management of one's life so that all the necessary goods
are coherently achieved, maintained, and enjoyed in a manner that is
appropriate for the individual human being.

Moral virtues are what form one's moral character. They are concerned with the use and control of one's emotions. Their aim, according to Veatch, is to help establish a harmony between what one ought
to desire and what one in fact does desire. Such virtues as integrity,
courage, temperance, and honesty thus assist the individual in using
practical wisdom to make the proper choices. However, there is more
to human flourishing than simply making proper choices. Human
flourishing is the enactment of *rational desire*. Properly choosing something is not separate from desire. Practical wisdom and moral virtue
must work together so that the individual human being acts with rational desire—that is, where one's emotions and intellect are one. This is
a way of being and a matter of character. It occurs only when it can be
said of a person interchangeably, "He is doing what he ought to do"
and "He is doing what he wants to do."

In true Aristotelian fashion, Veatch did not think that it was the
task of practical wisdom to develop *a priori* universal rules that dictate
either *the* proper balance (or weighting) of basic goods or *the* proper
emotional response to a situation. The contingent situation, the particular circumstances, and the individual him- or herself are always
relevant factors in determining the proper choice. What was clear for

Veatch was that the ethical life requires that individuals know them-selves and their situations and discover the proper balance and emo-tional response *for themselves.* After all, Aristotle did speak of "the mean relative to us."

Veatch's emphasis on the individual also had another dimension. Human flourishing must be attained through one's own efforts and cannot be the result of factors that are beyond one's control. Human flourishing is, as Veatch would remark in one of his later works, a "do-it-yourself job." There is no such thing as self-perfection if the indi-vidual human being is not the agent. Indeed, practical wisdom does not function without personal effort or exertion on the part of the individual. There is nothing automatic about it. Moral virtue leads to character, and character must be developed through the practice of morally virtuous activities.

Veatch's emphasis on the individual placed him in conflict with both the utilitarian rule-based approach to ethics as well as the Kantian notion of "universalizability." One cannot, for Veatch, attempt to de-velop ethical rules or principles that treat individuals as interchange-able, as if individuality did not matter morally. The individual does make a moral difference. Veatch's approach to ethics in the 1960s was in many ways preparing the philosophical world for the criticisms of impersonalism that would come later in the twentieth century. *Rational Man* was in several ways a harbinger of what later moral philosophers would call "virtue ethics."

Veatch argued in *Rational Man* that an appeal to human nature pro-vides the contemporary reader with knowledge of the basic goods of human flourishing, an awareness of the centrality of practical wisdom and moral virtue, and an appreciation of the importance of individual choice. Yet, such an appeal never provides a recipe by which one guides one's conduct. One cannot determine what one ought to do merely by appealing to an abstract understanding of human flourish-ing. Ethics is not an armchair art. Thus, Veatch's Aristotelian ethics is fundamentally opposed to this sort of ethical rationalism.

In a lively and trenchant way, Veatch sought to rehabilitate the natu-ral law tradition by showing that ethical knowledge can be based on human nature without requiring the adoption of a "one-size-fits-all" approach to human conduct. Human flourishing is not something monistic or simple, and it is always the good *for* some individual or other. Veatch allowed for different weightings of basic goods without supposing that human nature is irrelevant to ethical knowledge. He thus occupied the middle ground between Germain Grisez and John Finnis (and the so-called new natural law theorists who argue that ethics requires no ontological grounding) and the more traditionally minded natural law theorists (usually neoscholastic philosophers) who seemingly thought that one could "read-off" the proper course of conduct from an analysis of human nature alone. Veatch was certainly an advocate of natural law ethics, but his understanding of it was subtle and nuanced.

In *Rational Man,* Veatch met head-on those who sought to ground ethical knowledge simply in an appeal to desires or duty for duty's sake. The human good has to be more than doing merely what we feel like doing, and ethics must make some sort of difference as to how we live our lives. If it does neither, then quite simply why bother ourselves with ethics? Despite their standing in academe, such approaches to ethics really have nothing to offer the ordinary man or woman who is trying to find a worthwhile life or, at least, trying not to make a mess of it.

Veatch confronted vigorously those who believed that a justification for freedom and tolerance could be found by rejecting all moral standards. He noted that Mussolini's fascism was as much a legitimate inference from the rejection of moral standards as any call for human liberty. He made clear the glaring non sequitur in all attempts to recommend a course of conduct from the premise that "no course of action is really superior to any other." He also noted that, to the extent human beings choose one course of conduct over another, they manifest a preference that is inconsistent practically with the rejection of all moral standards. Veatch's criticisms of most postmodernism are equally trenchant.

Contrary to much prevalent thought, *Rational Man* was not written explicitly as a polemical response to William Barrett's widely read *Irrational Man* (1958). Veatch was concerned to show, by dusting off the insights of Aristotelian realist theory, that human beings do have an alternative to being irrational and that they do not face a meaningless and absurd existence. Philosophical realist that he was, Veatch argued that there is a sense and meaning to things and that the human mind can know this meaning. Knowing this does not require that one be Godlike or incapable of error. Yet, it does require openly and honestly facing oneself, and the world, and engaging thoroughly in the examination Socrates recommended so long ago.

Douglas B. Rasmussen
2002

An Annotated Bibliography of Henry B. Veatch's Major Works in Chronological Order

BOOKS

Intentional Logic: A Logic Based on Philosophical Realism
New Haven, Conn.: Yale University Press, 1952
This powerful work is fundamental to Veatch's thought and is at least as relevant today as when it first appeared. This work treats logic as Aristotle did—namely, as an *organon,* that is, as a tool for knowledge. It challenges many of the contemporary positions found in analytic philosophy regarding the nature of logic. From issues pertaining to the character of logical forms and relations to the alleged primacy of the analytic-synthetic account of propositions, this book argues that the failure to understand the intentional character of logic lies at the very heart of many of the basic confusions and problems of contemporary analytic philosophy.

Realism and Nominalism Revisited
Milwaukee: Marquette University Press, 1954
This tightly argued and clearly written work was the Aquinas Lecture for 1954 at Marquette University. Veatch took issue with Gottlob Frege's and W. V. O. Quine's characterizations of logic and accused both of resurrecting the ancient "problem of universals"—a problem for Veatch that had its solution in Aquinas' "moderate realism."

Logic as a Human Instrument
With Frank Parker. New York: Harper and Row, 1959
The work is for classroom use as a logic text, but it uses insights from *Intentional Logic* to explain concepts, propositions, and arguments. Chapter 1's discussion of the nature of signs is very important to understanding not only Veatch's thought but also philosophical realism in general. The discussion of the Aristotelian, as opposed to the Millean, account of induction is very instructive regarding some of the central issues in the so-called problem of induction.

Rational Man: A Modern Interpretation of Aristotelian Ethics
London and Bloomington: Indiana University Press, 1962. Translated by J. M. Garcia del la Mora as *Ética del ser racionel.* Barcelona, 1967

Two Logics: The Conflict between Classical and Neo-analytic Philosophy
Evanston, Ill.: Northwestern University Press, 1968
Veatch argued that the neo-analytic view of concepts and propositions is unable to provide a knowledge of what things are, while the neo-Aristotelian

view of concepts and propositions can provide such knowledge. In some ways, Veatch's discussion of neo-analytic philosophy predicted the deconstructionism of Stanley Fish and Richard Rorty. There are also important discussions of the differences between scientific and humanistic knowing, what essentialism is and is not, and the significance of fallibilism.

For an Ontology of Morals: A Critique of Contemporary Ethical Theory
Evanston, Ill.: Northwestern University Press, 1968
This sophisticated and important work does three things: (1) it contends that neo-analytic and existentialist ethics provide us with no recourse but ethical nihilism; (2) it argues that the Kantian philosophical device, the transcendental turn, ultimately provides no help to the analysts and existentialists; and (3) it defends the thesis that only an ontological turn in ethics can avoid ethical nihilism. The third thesis involves a fascinating account of goodness as an objective and natural, but also supervenient and relational, property as well as a defense of natural law ethics against utilitarianism and Kantian duty ethics.

Intentional Logic: A Logic Based on Philosophical Realism, 1970
Unaltered and unabridged reprint by Archon Books, Hamden, Conn.

Aristotle: A Contemporary Appreciation
London and Bloomington: Indiana University Press, 1974
Veatch was a lucid and learned mentor of Aristotle, and never more so than in this work, which provides marvelously clear accounts of Aristotle's doctrine of the four causes, the soul, and being qua being, along with introductory discussions of Aristotle's *Ethics, Politics,* and *Poetics.* Veatch argued that Aristotle is the philosopher of common sense *par excellence.*

Human Rights: Fact or Fancy?
Baton Rouge and London: Louisiana State University Press, 1985
This work holds that only a natural law ethics that bases itself on teleology can provide a ground for natural rights; neither a desire nor a duty ethics will suffice. Veatch's conception of the basic rights of life, liberty, and property is negative, not positive. Further, Veatch held that the common good of the political community has to be truly good for every individual. Thus, what the state could claim as its function on behalf of the common good was severely limited, since the human good for Veatch was never some "Platonic" form.

Swimming against the Current in Contemporary Philosophy: Occasional Papers and Essays
Studies in Philosophy and the History of Philosophy, vol. 20, ed. Jude P. Dougherty. Washington, D.C.: Catholic University Press of America, 1990
This collection includes many of Veatch's most important articles, especially from the 1980s. The views of such contemporary philosophers as Quine, Rorty, Alan Donagan, and Alan Gewirth come in for some important criticism. There are also discussions of the principle of universalizability, right reason, ethical egoism, natural rights, and libertarian political theory. Finally, there are essays on the value of humanistic learning and essays challenging John Finnis and the "new natural law theorists."

SELECTED ARTICLES

"Concerning the Ontological Status of Logical Forms"
    Review of Metaphysics 2 (1948): 40–64.
"Aristotelian and Mathematical Logic"
    The Thomist 13 (1950): 50–96.
"In Defense of the Syllogism"
    Modern Schoolman 26 (1950): 184–202.
"Basic Confusions in Current Notions of Propositional Calculi"
    The Thomist 14 (1951): 238–258.
"Discussion: Reply to Professor Copi"
    Philosophy and Phenomenological Research 11 (1951): 373–375.
"Formalism and/or Intentionality in Logic"
    Philosophy and Phenomenological Research 11 (1951): 348–365.
    The preceding articles express in different ways, and sometimes with greater
    detail than *Intentional Logic,* the nature of Veatch's complaint against so-called
    mathematical logic.
"On Trying to Say and Know What's What"
    Philosophy and Phenomenological Research 24 (1963): 83–96.
"The Truths of Metaphysics"
    Review of Metaphysics 17 (1964): 372–395.
"St. Thomas and the Question 'How are Synthetic Judgments a Priori Possible?'"
    Modern Schoolman 42 (1965): 239–263.
    The preceding articles take up an ongoing theme of Veatch's philosophical
    career—namely, the difference between the conception of the proposition
    in Aristotelian thought and that of contemporary analytic philosophy. These
    articles are worth reading if for no other reason than to appreciate Veatch's
    dialectical moves.
"Non-cognitivism in Ethics: A Modest Proposal for Its Diagnosis and Cure"
    Ethics 76 (1966): 102–116.
    This essay offers criticism of G. E. Moore's "open-question argument" and a
    clear discussion of Veatch's claim that goodness is a natural, but supervenient
    and relational, property.
"Kant and Aquinas: A Confrontation on the Contemporary Meta-ethical Field
of Honor"
    New Scholasticism 48 (1974): 73–99.
    This work discusses how Aquinas found it possible for the good to be an ob-
    ject of desire and so determine the will in the manner of reasons that serve
    to warrant or justify choices.
"The Rational Justification of Moral Principles: Can There Be Such a Thing?"
    Review of Metaphysics 29 (1975): 217–238.
    This essay considers the question, "Why be moral?" and argues that neither a
    duty ethics nor a desire-based ethics can provide a satisfactory answer. But if

goodness is an objective feature of things in the real world and also the object of desires and interests, then we can have both a reason and a motivation for being moral.

"On the Use and the Abuse of the Principle of Universalizability"

Proceedings of the American Catholic Philosophical Association 51 (1977): 162–170. This work distinguishes the principle of universalizability from impartialist and altruistic interpretations of it.

"Is Kant the Gray Eminence of Contemporary Ethical Theory?"

Ethics 90 (1980): 218–238.

Kant's influence in contemporary ethics is shown in this work to be the source of the egoism-altruism paradigm. Also, Aquinas' view of rational agency is contrasted to Kant's.

"A Non-Cartesian Meditation upon the Doctrine of Being in the Aristotelian Metaphysics"

In *Graceful Reason: Essays in Ancient and Medieval Philosophy Presented to Joseph Owens*, CSSR, ed. Lloyd P. Gerson, 75–100. Papers in Mediaeval Studies 4. Toronto: Pontifical Institute of Mediaeval Studies, 1983.

This essay offers a profound account of essence and substance in Aristotle's metaphysics. It also shows how the conception of logic used by most contemporary philosophers prevents them from understanding the central insight of Aristotle's metaphysics—namely, that individual things can actually *be* what they are as opposed to having their nature determined by some *tertium quid*.

"Modern Ethics, Teleology, and Love of Self"

The Monist 75 (1992): 52–70.

This essay provides an argument showing how an ethics of self-love, if teleologically construed, can be universalizable but not impersonal or agent-neutral.

Foreword

A few years ago there was published in this country an arresting book entitled *Irrational Man.* The aim of the author, Mr. William Barrett, was not to show that human beings are in fact irrational much of the time, perhaps most of the time. Every one has been so acutely aware of this for so long that it scarcely needs writing a book about. Instead, Mr. Barrett's purpose was to show that man has no alternative but to be irrational, since the situation in which human beings find themselves is essentially meaningless and absurd. To be rational presupposes that one can find some sense and meaning in things. But if things have no sense or meaning, what then?

The intent of the present essay is in no wise polemical, particularly not toward Mr. Barrett. But we are entitled to ask, before we settle for irrationality: "What does the alternative of trying to live rationally and intelligently really mean? What is it like to be rational?" In order to answer such a question one need not fall back on his own untutored experience; even if he is happy enough (or presumptuous enough) to draw on his own experience, it will scarcely be an original or novel experience. All of us who are products of Western culture have, either consciously or unconsciously, been to school to the Greeks, to Socrates, to Plato, and to Aristotle.

What follows, therefore, is an account of the ethics of rational man, an ethics that owes its inspiration and articulation largely to the *Nicomachean Ethics* of Aristotle. But this book is no scholarly treatise. Modern academic scholars in the field of Greek philosophy may be horrified at the cavalier way in which notions vaguely reminiscent of the Stagirite are here scrambled and twisted, pruned and amplified. For this the author makes no apology His purpose has been not to expound Aristotle but to use him in a modern effort to set forth and justify a rational system of ethics. Anyone who has read Aristotle's *Ethics* must have asked himself how those insights and ethical counsels that were so relevant to fourth-century Athens would apply in the cultural and moral situation of the present day. What would the precepts of Aristotle—or of Socrates and Plato—mean, how would they apply, what would they entail if one sought to live by them today?

With an objective that is thus practical and even personal, it becomes possible to explain, and perhaps to justify, certain other sins of omission and commission in what follows. From the standpoint of contemporary academic ethics this book is hopelessly out of step and out of fashion. To point the contrast we may quote the opening paragraphs of one of the more significant treatises on ethics to appear in the last few years:

> This book deals not with the whole of ethics, but with a narrowly specialized part of it. Its first object is to clarify the meaning of the ethical terms—such terms as "good," "right," "just," "ought," and so on. Its second object is to characterize the general methods by which ethical judgments can be proved or supported.
>
> Such a study is related to normative (or "evaluative") ethics in much the same way that conceptual analysis and scientific method are related to the sciences. One would not expect a book on scientific method to do the work of science itself; and one must not expect to find here any conclusions about what conduct is right or wrong. The purpose of an analytic or methodological study, whether of science or of ethics, is always indirect. It hopes to send others to their tasks with clearer heads and less wasteful habits of investigation. This necessitates a continual scrutiny of what these others are doing, or else analysis of meanings and methods will proceed in a vacuum; but it does not require the analyst, as such, to participate in the inquiry that he analyzes. In ethics any direct participation of this sort might have its dangers. It might deprive the analysis of its detachment and distort a relatively neutral study into a plea for some special code of morals. So although normative questions constitute by far the most important branch of ethics, pervading all of common-sense life, and occupying most of the professional attention of legislators, editorialists, didactic novelists, clergymen, and moral philosophers, these questions must here be left unanswered.

The present volume has the limited task of sharpening the tools which others employ.*

This book, however, does not attempt to sharpen any tools. It does not profess to stand outside ethics and merely to analyze its meanings and methods. Instead, it attempts precisely that "direct participation" in ethics which Mr. Stevenson warns "might have its dangers." It is true that the job that is here being undertaken may be such as to "deprive the analysis of its detachment." Still, one wonders whether, when the house is burning or the ship sinking, detachment is quite the proper attitude. I am even willing to admit that what follows will in a sense involve "a plea for some special code of ethics." But I would not like to admit that a special plea must necessarily involve special pleading.

I am not sure that the analogy really holds between what has come to be known as the philosophy or logic of science, involving analysis of the concepts and methods used in the sciences (as distinct from the sciences themselves), and what might be called the philosophy or logic or perhaps meta-ethics of ethics, involving the study of the logic and language of morals or ethics (as distinct from morals or ethics themselves).

I wonder too whether there may not be something slightly self-righteous in the usual pose of the contemporary ethical philosopher, who modestly claims to confine his attention entirely to questions of the language or logic of ethics, leaving all substantive ethical questions to "legislators, editorialists, didactic novelists, clergymen, and moral philosophers." It must be very reassuring to the complacency of the present-day professor of ethics to proclaim it beneath his scientific calling to give practical advice in the manner of an editorial writer or a clergyman. As for the philosophers of science, they show respect, not to say veneration, for the scientists. But the philosophers of ethics tend to regard anyone playing the role of moralist as no better than a "phony." As a result, that branch of ethics which in the foregoing quotation is dubbed "the most important" is the part which is most ne-

---

*Charles L. Stevenson, *Ethics and Language,* New Haven: Yale University Press, 1944, p. 1.

glected in today's academic world. Professors no longer profess it and students no longer study it.

Let it then be frankly acknowledged that this book will have to do with just such normative questions as the currently regnant intelligentsia has come to regard as not philosophically respectable. The reader need not be surprised if he fails to find here the kind of scholastic discussion that tends to divide — and, one is tempted to add, to conquer — latter-day professors of ethics in this country. Not that such discussions are not needed. But even if I had the competence for the undertaking, I should scarcely have the will for it. As a professor, one may relish controversy with other professors; as a teacher, one may needle and cajole one's students; but as a human being one feels a responsibility to engage in frank and open discussion with other human beings about those moral and ethical questions that have plagued thoughtful men of all ages. In what follows, therefore, my concern will be to consider philosophical difficulties and perplexities in common human terms, rather than in the technical terms of academic controversy.

Political and social questions are not dealt with in this book. It is the individual's responsibility to himself, not his responsibility to society, that is here being investigated. This omission is deliberate, and not merely for reasons of economy, but also for the sake of a much needed redressing of the balance. Nowadays most of us seem to have fallen into the habit of gauging a man's worth solely in terms of the contribution he makes to the community. We take it for granted that a big business executive is more important than a laborer, a famous surgeon than an ordinary housewife, a brilliant physicist than a laboratory assistant. But would we not all agree that however distinguished a public official or man of affairs may be, however signal his contributions to science or to the national economy, yet, considered just as a person, as a human being, our man of distinction may turn out to be far from admirable? There is no necessary correlation between a man's contribution to society and his worth as an individual. This book is concerned with a man's worth in himself, regardless of any utilitarian estimate that may be placed upon him in virtue of his services to the leviathan of modern society.

Nor does this book deal with religion or the relation of religion to ethics. It is not just in the popular mind that morals seem to be inseparably bound up with religious prohibitions and sanctions. Even in the academic mind, it passes almost for a truism that when one moves from theories about ethics to actual ethical convictions, the latter can be little more than matters of faith and belief, not matters of evidence and knowledge. But this book professes to be through and through a book of philosophy; therefore its argument must rely not on any appeals to revelation, but solely on what used to be known as the natural light of reason.

I believe that ethics can be based on evidence and that it is a matter of knowledge; but I do not claim that this is the whole story. However it may have been with a philosopher like Aristotle, most of us ordinary mortals cannot even know the good life, much less practice it, without some aid from a source outside ourselves. Such an association of ethics with religion is, I believe, entirely compatible with the sort of Aristotelian ethics presented here. But it is not this side of the story that I propose to tell. I wish to set forth a book simply on ethics, ethics without religion, if you will.

H. B. V.

Rational Man

1

In Quest of Ethical Knowledge

1. What is ethics?

Just what sort of enterprise is ethics? Is it the wearisome one of telling people what they ought or ought not to do? Or perhaps the gratuitous, even presumptuous, one of lecturing them on what the good
life for man must needs consist in? Surely no one but a fool would
let himself in for any such undertaking as this. Even the professors of
ethics nowadays have had the wit to avoid any semblance of preaching.
They would not for a minute consider it their business to instruct students in such time-honored themes as "the difference between right
and wrong," "the good life for man," or the obligation of being "for
God, for country, and for Yale." No, theirs, they would claim, is the
more modest, and, if you will, the more properly philosophical, task of
clarifying the meanings and uses of characteristic words and phrases
that occur in the language of morals and ethics. Thus a statement to
the effect that one ought to pay one's debts turns out to be an assertion of a different sort from either "v = gt" or "Jack Sprat could eat no
fat." It isn't like a straightforward statement of fact, and it isn't like a
law of nature either. Is it, then, more on the order of an explicit or implicit command to someone to do something? Or maybe it is an assertion of the existence of a somewhat mysterious, non-natural property
of obligatoriness which is held to attach to such courses of action as
paying your debts or speaking the truth.

With these and like questions as to the language of morals, the current academic study of ethics seems largely to concern itself. This may
be all to the good. To keep professors occupied with mere questions

of language, as distinct from questions of substance, could actually be very much in the public interest, many people might say. The only trouble is that to most people it must seem that ethics has to do with more than just the meanings of words and uses of language. Indeed, to the student who naïvely and ingenuously turns his attention to the study of ethics, it must surely seem that what he is seeking to find out is not so much what the word "good" means, as what the good life is, not whether the verb "ought" is more properly used in an imperative or an indicative sense, as whether he himself ought to do this or that. After all, for a man wanting to learn to drive a car, it would be a rather frustrating experience if his instructor consistently refused to tell him what to do, confining his remarks entirely to an analysis of the language used in the drivers' manuals and refraining from any comment as to whether the actual instructions of the manuals were to be followed or not.

Very well, then, if one feels that ethics has more to do than merely analyze the language of moral discourse, does that mean that in one's own discourses on ethics he will have to let himself in for edifying disquisitions on the good life, or perhaps for neat, well-packaged instructions on how to be good, in ten easy lessons? It is hard to imagine anything sillier, or more pretentious.

2. Why not consider ethics an art of living?

The comparison with learning to drive a car may prove to be unexpectedly apposite for an understanding of ethics. For what about such things as learning to live or learning how to be human? Are not these things that we have to learn how to do, just as we have to learn how to drive or to lay bricks or to keep accounts or to butcher hogs? It's true that words are somewhat ambiguous and misleading in this connection. Thus it will no doubt be remarked that as long as one remains alive, one does live; and if one belongs to the species "man" one can't very well help being a human being. In this sense, living or being human are not so much things that we learn how to *do*, as things that we either *are* or are not.

At the same time, it certainly makes sense to speak of living well, as contrasted with making a mess of one's life. Who is there who is not concerned, in some way or other and however he may express it, with some such thing as getting something out of life, achieving happiness, making the proper adjustment to life, being successful, or perhaps just simply getting along, or maybe even "living it up"? Moreover, whatever form this concern with our own lives may take, we surely recognize that in this enterprise of living we may, and probably will, make mistakes. But still we can always learn. Indeed, the very fact that we see that we do make mistakes means that we have thereby come to have at least some notion of what not making mistakes would be like. In other words, experience would seem to be a teacher in life, just as it is in business or in medicine or in driving a car.

Why not, then, suppose that from experience in life there can be developed something like an art of living, just as from human experience of various kinds there have developed the various arts of medicine, of managing property, of building bridges, of walking tightropes, and of driving cars? Carrying the analogy still further, just as no one is born a good doctor or bricklayer or orator or radio technician, but must first learn the requisite art or technique, so why not say that no one is born a good man, that one must first learn the art of living? Living well, in other words, is like driving well or trying a case well or performing an appendectomy well: it's an art or technique that one must master, a skill that one must acquire before one can do it well, or perhaps even do it at all.

3. But is living something that one can learn how to do?

At this point the reader may be saying to himself: "The whole idea of morals or ethics being an art comparable to the arts of medicine and engineering is simply preposterous. For unlike any of the genuine arts or techniques, any pretended art of living—supposing that it is legitimate even to use such a term—can be only a matter of opinion, and not a matter of knowledge. That it is better to perform a surgical operation in one way rather than another, or that it is better to construct a bridge using certain types of materials rather than others—these are judgments that can be put to the test and shown to be correct or incorrect. But how is one to test a judgment to the effect that the way of life in the so-called Free World is better than that in the Communist world? How could one ever establish objectively the correctness of a judgment to the effect that being honest with oneself is better than fooling or deluding oneself?"

4. The groves of academe: the divorce between learning and living

Supposing this to be the judgment of the reader, there is no denying the countless cold, hard facts that would seem to warrant even harsher judgments. Chief among these is the arresting and embarrassing fact of modern science and scholarship itself. For let's face it: modern learning does not have anything to do with living, or being learned with being human. That is to say, if there were such a thing as a genuine art of living, would not this mean that there would have to be a legitimate and recognized body of knowledge underlying such an art and making it possible? But where is one to find any such body of knowledge that could correspond to the art of living, in the way in which, say, modern physics corresponds to modern engineering? Suppose that one were to thumb through the voluminous printed course offerings of a modern college or university. Where would one find a course on how to live? And if one did find such a course, the conclusions one would draw would not be very complimentary to any department or school that presumed to dispense knowledge on any such topic as that.

Or look at the matter in this way, this time not with respect to areas of scientific and scholarly knowledge, but with respect to the scientists and scholars themselves: Is there any noticeable, to say nothing of any proper, correlation between what a man knows and what he is, that is, his character as a human being? Take modern physics again: does a man's skill and competence as a physicist have the slightest bearing on the kind of person he is? May a man not be a brilliant physicist and at the same time be mean and envious, or vain and conceited, or a false friend, or a Jew-baiter? I remember from student days in Heidelberg, just at the outset of the Nazi regime, hearing students talk of a distinguished professor of physics at the University who used to open his lectures with the threatening question: "Is there a Jew anywhere in the room?"

Nor need one imagine that the situation is so far different in the humanities from what it is in the sciences. There, too, the facts seem equally inescapable. A man may be an exceedingly estimable person in every way—a good companion, a loyal friend, a responsible citizen, a conscientious worker—and still be only a very mediocre Chaucerian scholar. And vice versa, no matter what a man's particular area of scholarly competence may be, whether in medieval history, or English literature, or musicology or whatnot—any and all such erudition seems to have no very direct bearing on the man's own worth and excellence as a human being.

The patent irrelevance of learning to life has become the occasion of some of the most pointed and amusing existentialist satire.

Such an abstract thinker, one who neglects to take into account the relationship between his abstract thought and his own existence as an individual, not careful to clarify this relationship to himself, makes a comical impression upon the mind even if he is ever so distinguished, because he is in process of ceasing to be a human being . . . such an abstract thinker is a duplex being: a fantastic creature who moves in the pure being of abstract thought, and on the other hand, a sometimes pitiful professorial figure which the former deposits, about as when one sets down a walking stick. When one reads the story of such a thinker's life (for his writings are perhaps excellent), one trembles to think of what it means to be a man. If a lace-maker were to produce ever so beautiful laces, it nevertheless makes one sad to contemplate such a poor stunted creature. And so it is a comical sight to see a thinker who in spite of all pretensions, personally existed like a nincompoop; who did indeed marry, but without knowing love or its power, and whose marriage must therefore have been as impersonal as his thought; whose personal life was devoid of pathos or pathological struggles, concerned only with the question of which university offered the best livelihood.[1]

*5. Is it not a paradox that "learning" seems
never to be learning how to live?*

The same point can be brought home even more forcibly when approached from a slightly different angle. In the case of those of us who have gone in for scientific or scholarly careers, suppose we simply ask ourselves, why pursue learning? C. P. Snow has one of his characters face up to this question, and his answer not only has the ring of truth; it is also exceedingly revealing:

> What had I told Audrey were the reasons why men did science? I should still say much the same, except that nowadays I should allow more for accident; many men become scientists because it happens to be convenient and they may as well do it as anything else. But the real urgent drives remain: there seemed to be three kinds. Three kinds of reason to give to oneself, that is. One can do science because one believes that practically and effectively it benefits the world. A great many scientists have had this as their chief conscious reason: for me it never was and at thirty it seemed more foolish than ten years before. . . .
>
> One can do science because it represents the truth. That or something like it, was the reason I had given in the past. So far as I had a conscious justification, it would always have been this. Yet it was not good enough, I thought, watching a red-sailed boat running between an island and the shore. Science was true in its own field; it was perfect within its restrictions. One selected one's data—set one's puzzle for oneself, as it were—and in the end solved the puzzle by showing how they fitted other data of the same kind. We know enough of the process now to see the quality of the results it can give us; we know, too, those sides of experience it can never touch. However much longer science is done, since it sets its own limits before it can begin, those limits must remain. It is rather as though one was avidly interested in all the countryside between this town and the next: one goes to science for an answer, and is given a road between the two. To think of this as the truth, to think of "the truth" at all as a unique ideal, seemed to me mentally naive to a degree. . . .
>
> One can also do science because one enjoys it. Naturally anyone

who believes wholeheartedly, either in its use or its truth, will at the same time enjoy it. Constantine, for example, gains more simple hedonistic enjoyment from research than most men from their chosen pleasures; and though he is the most devoted scientist I know, there are many men to whom enjoyment comes as a consequence of faith. But I think it is also possible to enjoy science without believing overmuch in its use, or having any views upon the value of its truths. Many people like unravelling puzzles. Scientific puzzles are very good ones, with reasonable prizes. So that either without examining the functions of science, being indifferent to them or taking them for granted, a number of men go in for research as they would for law; living by it, obeying its rules, and thoroughly enjoying the problem-solving process. That is a perfectly valid pleasure; among them you can find some of the most effective of scientists.[2]

In the context of our present investigation, the interesting thing about these reasons for doing science, or, more generally, for devoting one's life to scientific and scholarly research, lies not so much in what such reasons explicitly affirm, as in what they fail to mention or even hint at. Isn't it significant that none of the reasons here given for the pursuit of knowledge has anything to do with what knowledge can do for the person or character of the knower himself? After all, one's life as a scientist can be of the greatest benefit to mankind, it can even be a life devoted to the pursuit of truth for its own sake, yes, it can be a life taken up with doing precisely what one most enjoys doing; and yet none of these activities or achievements in a life of science and learning provides any guarantee that the one who lives such a life will be anything but pompous and foolish, perhaps dull and drab, a mere "hollow man," in fact. Why, then, shouldn't one seek knowledge precisely for the reason that through such knowledge one may learn how to avoid being a hollow man? Perhaps such knowledge will help him discover what Pope once felicitously termed "that secret to each fool that he's an ass." But somehow, modern scientific and scholarly knowledge does not seem to lend itself to any such enterprise.

Why shouldn't it, though? For it has not always been so with knowledge. On the contrary, in the case of Socrates, for example, the pursuit of knowledge was for no other purpose than that of finding out how to live. "Know thyself" was the inscription from the Oracle of Delphi which Socrates took as the motto of his own quest for knowledge. In fact, as is well known, he completely gave over his own earlier interest in the cosmos and devoted himself entirely to this pursuit of a knowledge which he called self-knowledge. Not only that, but he constantly exhorted his fellow Athenians that they turn from their customary pursuits and occupy themselves with themselves and with the good of their own souls:

> . . . and while I have life and strength I shall never cease from the practice and teaching of philosophy, exhorting any one whom I meet and saying to him after my manner: You, my friend—a citizen of the great and mighty and wise city of Athens,—are you not ashamed of heaping up the greatest amount of money and honour and reputation, and caring so little about wisdom and truth and the greatest improvement of the soul, which you never regard or heed at all?
>
> . . . I say again that daily to discourse about virtue, and of those other things about which you hear me examining myself and others, is the greatest good of man, and that the unexamined life is not worth living. . . .[3]

Moreover, when one stops to think about it, it appears that nearly all of the great world religions have likewise had for their central concern the disclosure to men of what one might designate quite simply as the way to live, the very word "way" being itself peculiarly significant and recurrent in this connection. Did not Christ declare, "I am the way, the truth and the life"? And likewise, in both Taoism and Confucianism the central preoccupation is with the Tao or the "way." In Buddhism, it is the "path," the noble eightfold path.

6. Is there no escaping this paradox?

What are we to make of all this? Are we to say that the whole of modern academic learning has somehow taken a wrong turning, that instead of being concerned with finding for us and demonstrating to us the way we should live, it has let itself be beguiled into pursuing a type of knowledge that has no relevance to us as human beings, or, better, no relevance to the knower, i.e., to the scientist and scholar himself? Or must we say that it is Socrates who was mistaken, rather than our modern scholars and scientists, that the entire Socratic quest for a knowledge which, to use a theological term, would be a "saving" knowledge, which would actually provide the knower himself with a vision of the way, the truth, and the life—that this Socratic quest was both misdirected and hopeless? Perhaps Socrates' mistake consisted precisely in his assumption that self-knowledge in his sense could actually be a matter of knowledge, that it would be possible for human beings through investigation and reflection to discover the way in which they should live. Continuing in the same vein, we might further remark that such a thing as the "way" might be revealed to a man in a religious context, as something that he might take on faith; but that it is anything that one can *know* in any of the usual senses of "know"— this would seem to be quite out of the question, to judge from the example of present-day academic knowledge.

7. A currently acceptable and dangerously uncritical way out: a knowledge of behavior

However, there is another facet to this whole question of the possibility of genuine ethical or moral knowledge, on which modern science and technology can perhaps shed a certain light. It will be remembered that at the outset of our discussion, the suggestion was thrown out that perhaps morals and ethics might be understood on the analogy of the various arts and techniques, that just as one has to learn how to walk or to read or to lay brick, so also one has to learn how to live and to be human. But no sooner do we reflect a little on the example of modern technology, than it begins to look as if the application of scientific knowledge were the very last thing that could serve as a model for the sort of thing which we want to call moral or ethical knowledge.

If such moral or ethical knowledge must needs involve a knowledge of oneself, in Socrates' sense—a "relating of one's abstract thought to one's own existence as an individual," to paraphrase the earlier quoted phrase from Kierkegaard[4]—surely this is something that modern technology never does, and is in principle incapable of doing. True, if we take loosely enough the somewhat fatuous phrase, "the relevance of knowledge to life," there is no doubt that modern technology provides a truly amazing example of the relevance of knowledge to life. For just think of the human needs and the human wants that can now be fulfilled in modern industrial society and that were simply incapable of being fulfilled in anything like the same degree or with anything like the same expertness in other ages of the world's history.

Yet what is needed for ethics is knowledge not of how to control nature, but of how to control oneself.

But interestingly enough, no sooner does one, in the spirit of modern technology, begin to address oneself to the task of controlling the human self, than one tends to turn the human self into just one more object among others in the natural world; and before one is through, one will be devising schemes for manipulating and controlling human selves, much as one manipulates and controls rats, fruit flies, and coal tar products. Not only do human selves cease to be selves in such a context, being treated as no more than just so many natural objects, but also—and this is even more serious, so far as ethics is concerned— the original enterprise of controlling oneself is lost sight of completely, and our would-be expert in how to live turns out to be not a master of his own life, but only a master in conditioning and controlling the lives of others.

We have but to turn to Gabriel Marcel to read a very revealing account of how all of us tend to view our fellow human beings, once we fall into the current habit of considering ways and means of applying modern scientific knowledge to the conduct of life, after the manner of modern technology.

> The characteristic feature of our age seems to me to be what might be called the misplacement of the idea of function, taking function in its current sense which includes both the vital and the social functions.
>
> The individual tends to appear both to himself and to others as an agglomeration of functions. As a result of deep historical causes, which can as yet be understood only in part, he has been led to see

himself more and more as a mere assemblage of functions, the hier-archical interrelation of which seems to him questionable or at least subject to conflicting interpretations.

Marcel then goes on to mention first the so-called vital functions, after this the social functions—"those of the consumer, the producer, the citizen, etc."—and finally the psychological functions. He then con-tinues:

> So far we are still dealing only with abstractions, but nothing is easier than to find concrete illustrations in this field.
>
> Travelling on the Underground, I often wonder with a kind of dread what can be the inward reality of the life of this or that man employed on the railway—the man who opens the doors, for in-stance, or the one who punches the tickets. Surely everything both within him and outside him conspires to identify this man with his functions—meaning not only with his functions as worker, as trade union member or as voter, but with his vital functions as well. The rather horrible expression "time table" perfectly describes his life. So many hours for each function. Sleep too is a function which must be discharged so that the other functions may be exercised in their turn. The same with pleasure, with relaxation; it is logical that the weekly allowance of recreation should be determined by an expert on hygiene; recreation is a psycho-organic function which must not be neglected any more than, for instance, the function of sex. We need go no further; this sketch is sufficient to suggest the emer-gence of a kind of vital schedule; the details will vary with the coun-try, the climate, the profession, etc., but what matters is that there is a schedule.
>
> It is true that certain disorderly elements—sickness, accidents of every sort—will break in on the smooth working of the system. It is therefore natural that the individual should be overhauled at regu-lar intervals like a watch (this is often done in America). The hospi-tal plays the part of the inspection bench or the repair shop. . . .
>
> As for death, it becomes, objectively and functionally, the scrap-ing of what has ceased to be of use and must be written off as total loss.[5]

Such a tendency to disintegrate one's fellow man into a mere assemblage of functions seems to be the inevitable accompaniment of our efforts to apply our scientific knowledge in the management of men's lives. But it must not be supposed that such a pulverization and disintegration must necessarily lead to the individual's unhappiness. On the contrary, Marcel's "man in the Underground" may well be the most contented and self-satisfied of men, perhaps even distressingly so. For as Huxley has dourly observed:

> There is, of course, no reason why the new totalitarianisms should resemble the old. Government by clubs and firing squads, by artificial famine, mass imprisonment and mass deportation, is not merely inhumane (nobody cares much about that nowadays); it is demonstrably inefficient—and in an age of advanced technology, inefficiency is the sin against the Holy Ghost. A really efficient totalitarian state would be one in which the all-powerful executive of political bosses and their army of managers control a population of slaves who do not have to be coerced, because they love their servitude. To make them love it is the task assigned, in present-day totalitarian states, to ministries of propaganda, newspaper editors and schoolteachers. But their methods are still crude and unscientific.[6]

8. Must we abandon the hope that ethics can be an art or a science?

But enough of this. What more is needed to show the folly and futility of trying to regard ethics as an art of living? So far from morals and ethics being in any way like the arts, it would now seem that the very idea of applying knowledge to life, in the manner of art or technology, would be absolutely ruinous to ethics. Instead of human beings leading examined lives as was envisaged by Socrates, any so-called art of living seems to lead to a situation in which human beings would become like so many cattle, herded and tended by various behavioral engineers and experts on living.

Why say more? Why not just acknowledge that there is no use pretending to any so-called moral or ethical knowledge? Socrates' project of an ethical knowledge that would be a self-knowledge seems completely out of line with our modern conception of knowledge, as this manifests itself in present-day science and scholarship. And as for the project of an art of living or an art of being human, comparable to the other arts and techniques, this would appear to be not merely futile, when viewed in the light of modern technology, but actually dangerous and wrong-headed.

Besides, isn't it a truism nowadays that morals and ethics are relative matters, that is to say, matters of opinion, not of knowledge? Or perhaps it might be more accurate to say that ethical relativism has become almost a *sine qua non* of the educated man, a sort of badge of the modern intellectual. One can still, perhaps, venture with impunity to admire examples of courage or integrity or decency, but one can hardly stand up and claim to know what is right and what is wrong without being laughed out of court, or at least out of a cocktail party.

9. Back to Methuselah and down with relativism

Perhaps there are worse fates. At any rate, I must assert unequivocally that I for one think that it *is* possible for men to know what is right and what is wrong. I would even go so far as to say that to assert anything else can only lead one into a quite untenable, even if often unnoticed, inconsistency. Ethical relativism, in other words, is, I believe, not just an indefensible position in philosophy; it is untenable in life itself.

To the end, however, of bringing off a full-dress refutation of ethical relativism, we should perhaps first take time to consider briefly just what the sources are of such an attitude toward ethics. If I mistake not, these sources are two, the one involving what might be called factual considerations, the other logical or linguistic considerations.

The so-called factual considerations are in a way so obvious in this day of higher education and academic sophistication as scarcely to deserve mention: it is a fact that men's moral and ethical judgments do seem to be relative to their civilization, their culture, their social class, their physical environment, yes, even to the biological and psychological dispositions of the individuals themselves. Nor is this fact attested to merely by the data of anthropology and sociology. In addition, countless psychological tests have been devised, the results of which appear to confirm unquestionably the relativity of men's value judgments.

Despite this impressive array of seemingly incontrovertible evidence, there is at least one respect in which this evidence is not conclusive. The mere fact of diversity in human moral standards does not in principle preclude the possibility of at least some of these standards being correct and others incorrect. For instance, consider a somewhat analogous situation in the modern natural sciences. It would not be difficult to show that in the course of the world's history theories of the physical universe have been almost as many and as varied and as relative as systems of morals and ethics. The ancient Egyptians doubtless gave entirely different explanations of physical change from those offered by contemporary physicists. And for all I know the astronomy of the ancient Babylonians was as different from that of the Chinese in the Ming dynasty as the Ptolemaic astronomy of medieval Europe is different from the astronomy of the present-day Einsteinian universe. Yet no one would conclude from such evidence that there is no basis in fact for a real science of physics or astronomy. Why, then, from the mere diversity of moral codes and systems of ethics, do we tend to conclude that morals and ethics cannot be genuine arts or sciences having a real basis in fact?

One might reply to this that while in former times theories of the physical universe were no doubt a relative matter, being mere idle speculations, determined by the peculiar prejudices of the age, the class, the culture, or the particular astronomer or physicist, in the modern period all this has changed: scientific theories now have a truly objective basis, as witness the extraordinary unanimity of scientists the world over. That is to say, no matter what the culture or the country or the economic system in which the modern scientist lives, he can still, as a scientist, understand and appreciate the achievements of other scientists everywhere.

This fact of comparative unanimity among scientists at present might provide at least some ground for supposing that science had at last been put on an objective basis, while morals or ethics had not; but even so, such evidence is still not really conclusive. To suppose that it was would be tantamount to holding that the determination of truth in science is no more than an affair of counting noses among scientists. And one could then go on to argue that since a plebiscite among moralists would yield nothing like the impressive results of a plebiscite among scientists, the palm of knowledge would have to be accorded to science, whereas ethics could claim to be no more than a matter of opinion.

10. The logical difficulties of claiming a factual knowledge in matters of ethics

The mere fact of diversity in moral and ethical opinion does not suffice to prove the impossibility in principle of moral and ethical knowledge: the whole world might be wrong and a single individual right. However, the case for ethical relativism need not rest on mere factual considerations; on the contrary, there are any number of considerations of a very different sort that lie ready at hand for the defense of such relativism. For it has become almost a dogma of the current intellectual scene to suppose that a radical distinction must always be drawn between facts and values, between "is" and "ought," between the real and the ideal. Since ethics by definition must presumably concern itself with values, as contrasted with facts, the conclusion seems inescapable that ethics is without objective or factual basis. Indeed, given these presuppositions, ethics has nothing to do with the real order, but only with the ideal—with what ought to be, rather than with what is.

In further confirmation of this conclusion, one has only to consider the logical difficulty, not to say impossibility, of ever establishing a normative or ethical judgment. For so far as empirical evidence goes, this is always evidence of what is so, of what actually is the case. But the ideal, or that which only *ought* to be, is in principle never observable. Even if it be supposed that in a given instance the ideal has not remained a mere ideal, but has actually been realized, it would still seem that its character of being ideal would be something quite above and apart from its actual properties.

For is it not true that scientific descriptions of actual things and events in the real world never seem to take account of whether these natural happenings are right or wrong, good or bad? Thus that water flows downhill may be taken to be a fact of the natural world. But that it is right or wrong, or good or bad, that water should behave in this way—any such consideration of a moral or ethical nature seems not only irrelevant in this connection, but downright silly.

For that matter, even the social sciences and sciences dealing with human behavior usually pride themselves on being scrupulous in their objectivity; and this is interpreted to mean that they refrain from any and all value judgments. An economist may study the phenomenon of slave labor, pointing out the various consequences of employing this means of production, and whether and under what circumstances such forced labor might or might not contribute to greater national productivity. But as to whether human slavery is right or wrong, morally defensible or indefensible—on this subject, while it might be hoped that as a human being the economist would have his private opinion, as an economist he can only protest that he has no objective knowledge one way or the other. Likewise, in anthropology, sociology, and psychology, the distinction is constantly being made between describing human behavior in one's role as a scientist and passing judgment upon such behavior in one's role as a person or as a citizen, the former being in the nature of objectively verifiable knowledge, whereas the latter is held to be no more than mere personal, private opinion.

One may deplore this ethical neutrality of modern science and complain that it has the effect of making scientists pander alike to dictators and to democracies. Be this as it may, how is one to get round the fact that value judgments do seem to be of a very different logical type from factual judgments? There is no way in which they can be objectively tested and verified. Nor does it seem possible even to make it intelligible just how the values which are ascribed to things can actually inhere in the things to which they are ascribed. Things are what they are objectively and in fact, but the values which they are said to have, they apparently can have only in the minds of the persons who judge them to be valuable.

Little wonder, then, that the moral or ethical dimension of things is not amenable to scientific investigation or verification. Be the facts what they may, one can neither find values in them nor infer values from them. And as for what is so being tantamount to what ought to be so, the "is" never provides the slightest clue as to any kind of an "ought." The two belong to logically quite different orders, and never the twain shall meet.

11. The refutation of relativism

Must all ethics, then, be written off as a hollow sham? Perhaps not. For the traditional disciplines of philosophy have a way of outdoing even old soldiers: they not only "never die"; they don't even "fade away." And so it may well prove to be with ethics.

Isn't there, indeed, some way in which the current criticisms of ethics can be met and answered, so as to rehabilitate the subject once more and make it a respectable scientific discipline? To this end, let us again remind ourselves of just what the thrust of these criticisms was. Briefly, it was to the effect that ethical judgments are ultimately without any basis in fact. Hence any and all human convictions as to what is right or wrong, good or bad, cannot possibly be other than relative and arbitrary.

Very well; but let us consider for a moment what would be the probable consequences of such a relativistic destruction of ethics. Offhand, it might be supposed that no sooner had men become convinced that morals and ethics were without foundation and that their various prohibitions and prescriptions were no longer binding, than the lid would be off and all hell would break loose. Certainly it is not hard to imagine how, at least with certain individuals, this might be the consequence of ethical relativism. For example, take a teen-age youth with normal sex impulses, whose strict upbringing had led him to believe that sex relations outside marriage are evil and wrong. Comes now an up-to-date moral philosopher who succeeds in convincing the young man that all such moral restraints stem merely from his Puritan upbringing and hence are quite without justification; indeed, they are but relative to this old-fashioned and now outmoded religious culture. Is it hard to imagine what effects such new-found convictions will have upon our young friend's consequent behavior?

One has only to reflect a bit, however, to realize that an excited casting off of all restraints is not a necessary or inevitable consequence of becoming convinced of the truth of ethical relativism. If it is true that all moral norms and standards of value are relative and, in this sense, arbitrary, it follows that no one set of values is superior to any other: all are equally good, or equally worthless, however one may prefer to express it. But viewed in this light, lust begins to appear as having really no more to recommend it than chastity, nor drunkenness than sobriety, nor prodigality than thrift. More generally, indeed, it begins to look as if a complete freedom from all the lets and hindrances of social convention would not really be any better than obedience and conformity. Accordingly, the wearied moral skeptic, who decides that it is less trouble after all simply to go along with everyone else and abide by the moral standards of the community, is being just as consistent—or inconsistent—in his ethical relativism as is the rebellious and hot-blooded youth whose impulsive reaction to relativism is to regard it as a free passport to wine, women, and song.

Nor are these the only variants on the possible consequences of ethical relativism. One has but to look at that very readable and plausible little book of the American anthropologist, Dr. Ruth Benedict. Entitled *Patterns of Culture,* the book attempts to exploit some of the wealth of modern anthropological research in support of a thesis of thoroughgoing ethical relativism. After all, Dr. Benedict argues, different human cultures, with their widely varying patterns, are to be regarded as "travelling along different roads in pursuit of different ends, and these ends and these means in one society cannot be judged in terms of those of another society, because essentially they are incommensurable."[7]

What may we suppose to be the consequences of such a recognition of relativism in the eyes of Professor Benedict? Oddly enough, as she views the matter, ethical relativism offers to human beings neither an invitation to license nor the tired counsels of skeptical pessimism; instead, it provides an impressive object lesson in tolerance.

> The truth of the matter is rather that the possible human institutions and motives are legion, on every plane of cultural simplicity or complexity, and that wisdom consists in a greatly increased tolerance toward their divergencies. No man can thoroughly participate in any culture unless he has been brought up and has lived

according to its forms, but he can grant to other cultures the same significance to their participants which he recognizes in his own.[8]

And in her final chapter Professor Benedict seems to turn moralist herself, sternly lecturing her readers that: "Just as we are handicapped in dealing with ethical problems so long as we hold to an absolute definition of morality,* so we are handicapped in dealing with human society so long as we identify our local normalities with the inevitable necessities of existence."[9] And so on, right up to the final eloquence of her concluding sentences:

> The recognition of cultural relativity carries with it its own values, which need not be those of the absolutist philosophies. It challenges customary opinions and causes those who have been bred to them acute discomfort. It rouses pessimism because it throws old formulae into confusion, not because it contains anything intrinsically difficult. As soon as the new opinion is embraced as customary belief, it will be another trusted bulwark of the good life. We shall arrive then at a more realistic social faith, accepting as grounds of hope and as new bases for tolerance the coexisting and equally valid patterns of life which mankind has created for itself from the raw materials of existence.[10]

While we are still bathing in the gentle warmth of such noble anthropological sentiments, it may be instructive to turn right around and expose ourselves to some rather more hard and gutsy utterances of

---

*A remark might be made in passing on Professor Benedict's use of the word "absolute," in speaking of an "absolute definition of morality." It is not unusual for ethical relativists to label their opponents "absolutists," the implication being that claims to absolutism in knowledge are about as fantastic and old-fashioned as claims to absolutism in monarchy. Nor is there any doubt that, linguistically, when one searches for a word that one can conveniently oppose to "relative," the only word that readily comes to mind is "absolute." And yet it is interesting that, so far as scientific knowledge is concerned, no one nowadays would venture to say that such knowledge was a purely relative matter. But does anyone for this reason consider that scientific knowledge is an absolute knowledge, or that scientists themselves are absolutists? And if scientists can enjoy an immunity from the dilemma of relativism or absolutism, why may not moral philosophers as well?

that late great master of cynicism and bombast, Benito Mussolini. Indeed, Mussolini's words (written in 1921) might also serve as an ironic commentary on Professor Benedict's preaching of tolerance on the text of relativism:

> In Germany relativism is an exceedingly daring and subversive theoretical construction (perhaps Germany's philosophical revenge which may herald the military revenge). In Italy, relativism is simply a fact. . . . Everything I have said and done in these last years is relativism by intuition. . . . If relativism signifies contempt for fixed categories and men who claim to be the bearers of an objective, immortal truth . . . then there is nothing more relativistic than Fascist attitudes and activity. . . . From the fact that all ideologies are of equal value, that all ideologies are mere fictions, the modern relativist infers that everybody has the right to create for himself his own ideology and to attempt to enforce it with all the energy of which he is capable.[11]

But why bother with further examples? These suffice to indicate that however plausible and even unanswerable the evidence would appear to be in support of a purely relativistic attitude in ethics, yet as soon as one asks what meaning and import such an attitude would have for one's own life and conduct, the answers turn out to be perplexingly confused and ambiguous. For one person, relativism means rebellion and libertinism; for another, conservatism and conformity. For one, it implies a greater tolerance and understanding of one's fellow men; for another, it justifies the most ruthless intolerance and the arbitrary imposing of one's own will upon others.

To make matters even worse, the consequences of such relativism are not only ambiguous, but also on closer scrutiny each of them turns out to involve a curious internal inconsistency. To return for a moment to Professor Benedict, is it not strange that having begun by proclaiming the utter relativity of all standards of value, she ends by preaching the gospel of tolerance? Presumably, if Professor Benedict is to remain faithful to her own principles, she must recognize that the value of tolerance is strictly relative to the particular cultural background which happens to have been her own. But suppose someone from a different cultural background has been brought up to believe that tolerance is not a virtue, but rather a sign of folly and weakness, the wise and courageous course being one of strict intolerance toward all divergencies from one's own cultural norm. What could Miss Benedict say to this? She could hardly disagree with such an advocate of intolerance, or criticize him for being mistaken, for this would be tantamount to judging the values of one society in terms of those of another. In fact, any such criticism would reflect that very spirit of intolerance toward peoples of other societies and cultures which Miss Benedict herself has made such a point of condemning. On the other hand, Miss Benedict could no more agree with such a hypothetical advocate of intolerance than she could disagree. For to agree would mean that she was conceding the superiority of the values of intolerance over those of tolerance—a stand which would doubtless convict her not merely of inconsistency, but of hypocrisy.

The predicament in which we have sought to place Professor Benedict is really not one of her own making, but is—in part at least—an inescapable predicament of anyone and everyone who would be a relativist in matters of ethics. For we might as well come right out now and unmask the battery from which we have been bombarding the various positions of relativism. As we see it, ethical relativism in any form is a radically inconsistent and thoroughly untenable position to try to hold in philosophy.

It is important to fix the precise nature of the inconsistency of such relativism. Unlike what might be called general relativism, or out-and-out philosophical skepticism, ethical relativism is not inconsistent in its very statement and formulation. When general philosophical skepticism is reduced to its simplest and crudest terms, the skeptic's position comes down to assertions of this sort: "I know that no one knows anything" or "The truth is that truth is unattainable." Assertions such as this are manifest self-contradictions.* That is why it may quite justly be said that any position of thoroughgoing relativism or skepticism in

---

*I am disregarding here the so-called type difficulties which have led some modern logicians to regard such statements as being not so much self-contradictory as improperly formed and hence not proper statements at all.

philosophy is untenable even in theory: the position cannot even be formulated and stated without contradiction.

On the other hand, when the relativism in question is simply a relativism in regard to matters of ethics and not in regard to human knowledge generally, there does not seem to be the same inconsistency. For one can perfectly well assert without any manifest contradiction such things as "I know that, when it comes to questions of ethics, no one knows anything"; or "The truth is that truth about values or about distinctions between right and wrong and good and evil, etc., is unattainable." Here, obviously, there is no logical inconsistency, i.e., no inconsistency in the very formulation of the position of ethical relativism itself.

But although there is no logical inconsistency, there is what one might call a practical inconsistency. Take the case of any convinced ethical relativist like Professor Benedict or the teen-age youth or Mussolini. If the foregoing analysis be correct, there is no inconsistency involved in his merely holding or subscribing to a position of relativism as such. The only trouble is that no human being can stop with just having convictions, he also has to live and to act. But to act is to choose and to choose is to manifest some sort of preference for one course of action over another. However, to manifest any such human preference means that, consciously or unconsciously, implicitly or explicitly, one has made a judgment of value as to which course of action is the better or the wiser or the more suitable or preferable. But what kind of a standard of value could the ethical relativist employ in making such judgments? The whole point of his relativism lies precisely in the fact that he intends to challenge the validity of any and every standard of value. On what possible basis, then, can the relativist act and choose and manifest his preference for doing one thing rather than another?

Caught up in such a predicament, the relativist no doubt may try to reason his way out in some such manner as this. He may try to employ his very relativism and skepticism in regard to all standards of value as if it were itself a kind of standard of value. Thus we can imagine him saying to himself, in effect: "Since all standards of value are utterly without foundation, since no way of life or course of action is really superior to any other, then the sensible thing for me to do is

1. to cultivate an attitude of greater tolerance toward the various modes of life and patterns of behavior that men have chosen for themselves (Miss Benedict), or
2. to create my own set of values and attempt to enforce them with all the energy of which I am capable (Mussolini), or
3. to throw off all moral standards and norms of conduct and simply follow the lead of my impulses and inclinations (the liberated youth), or
4. to go along with the crowd and merely abide by the standards of the community of which I am a member, this being the line of least resistance and the one least likely to get me into trouble and difficulty (the cynical skeptic)."

But unhappily, assuming that the relativist does reason in some such way as this, it is obvious that the reasoning will not bear scrutiny even for an instant. For the fallacy is only too transparent in the attempted inference from the utter relativity of all moral norms and standards of value to a course of action which the relativist considers to be the wisest and most sensible for him to follow under the circumstances. For "wiser" and "more sensible" in this connection are but synonyms for "better" or "preferable." Hence, put in its baldest form, the relativist's reasoning amounts to no more than a glaring *non sequitur:* "Since no course of action is really better or superior to any other, I conclude that the better course of action for me to follow would be thus and so."

Little wonder that under these circumstances the practical consequences of ethical relativism should be as various and as conflicting as those exemplified by Miss Benedict and Signor Mussolini. Indeed, in the light of the analysis we have just carried out, we can now see that no matter what practical implications one seeks to derive from such relativism, they are bound to involve one in an inconsistency, there being no possible way in which the very denial of all standards of better and worse can itself be transformed into a kind of standard of better and worse. Nor is there any way in which the relativist can avoid the practical inconsistency of his position. For however convinced he may be of the relativity of all norms and standards of choice, he must nonetheless act and make choices himself. Indeed, even if *per impossibile* he were to try to evade ever having to make any sort of a choice, his policy of evasion would itself be the result of a kind of choice and would involve at least an implicit judgment to the effect that such a course of evasion was the best one or the least bad one for him to pursue under the circumstances.

One is almost tempted to suggest that there is no other way for an ethical relativist to escape the inconsistency of his position than by having the good fortune to be struck dead, or to be rendered *non compos mentis,* immediately upon becoming convinced of the truth of relativism, and before he has had a chance to make so much as a single choice or decision on the basis of his new-found convictions. Such, however, would seem to be a cruel fate to wish even upon an ethical relativist, and surely a high price to pay merely for consistency. Wouldn't it be easier for him to forgo his relativism altogether?

2

The Examined Life: Back to Socrates and Aristotle

1. Reorientation and new departure

Our first chapter may have left the reader with an impression of confusion worse confounded. Ethical knowledge, it seems, although it may be something devoutly to be wished for, is at the same time something hardly to be realized, not only in practice, but even in principle. Indeed, for anyone to claim that in the present day men actually do possess an art of living comparable to the arts of war, of medicine, or of metallurgy would be simply preposterous. What's more, there appears to be no way either in fact or in logic for us ever to get from a scientific knowledge of the facts of human behavior to any sort of moral or ethical knowledge of what might be called the "oughts" of human behavior. The very project of developing such a thing as a scientifically grounded art or skill of living and of being human seems to be hopelessly impossible.

And yet no sooner did we expose the apparent impossibility of ethical knowledge than we appeared suddenly to turn the tables and to argue that any denial of the possibility of ethical knowledge is itself impossible. Or if not exactly impossible logically, such a denial of ethical knowledge was at least seen to lead into what, for want of a better term, we chose to call a practical or existential inconsistency.

Where, then, do we go from here? Well, suppose we try to go in a direction in which almost no other ethical writers of the present day are wont to go. Suppose we take quite seriously this seemingly inescapable human situation in which we human beings find ourselves and according to which we cannot very well deny the possibility of ethical knowledge without thereby involving ourselves in a practical or existential inconsistency. And since we cannot avoid an assumption as to the possibility of ethical knowledge, let us make a virtue of necessity and assume it. Having made the assumption that such knowledge is possible, let us attempt to convert the possibility into an actuality by showing what it actually means to be a human being and what being human does in fact consist in. In this way, we shall perhaps be able to sketch out at least the rudiments of a genuine art of living.

Such a procedure is not popular among contemporary ethical writers. On the contrary, it just isn't done. It has become commonplace today to consider that the only proper starting point for ethics is not the possibility of ethical knowledge, but, ironically enough, its utter impossibility. If this seems paradoxical, remember what we have already been at pains to point out, that a general attitude of relativism and skepticism in regard to matters of ethics is simply taken for granted as part of the heritage of modern man. Nor is it merely taken for granted; for as we have seen, it rests on the twin foundation stones of: (1) the seemingly obvious relativity, simply as a matter of fact, of all known moral norms and standards of value, and (2) the equally obvious neutrality—this time as a matter of principle—of all actual facts and occurrences within the real world.

Be it noted also that although we have tried to show that such an attitude of ethical relativism and skepticism is untenable, because inconsistent, we have not as yet done anything in the way of directly undermining its two foundation stones: the factual relativity of moral norms and the logical impossibility of grounding such norms on scientifically observable facts. Nor do we even propose to do anything of the sort, at least not just at present. Rather our procedure will be simply to leave these difficulties on one side, in the assurance that there must be some way of meeting them, however much we ourselves may be in the dark as to what this way is. The ground for this assurance lies in what should by now be a perfectly clear awareness that one cannot with consistency be a thoroughgoing relativist or skeptic in regard to matters of ethics.

2. *Does not man have a natural end?*

Given the assurance that ethical knowledge is at least possible, let's damn the torpedoes and sail right into the question of what we do and can know in ethics, of what is best for us as men, and of what we ought and need to do in order to be truly human. This enterprise of determining what our human purposes and goals are may well prove to be less difficult than one might at first suppose. Setting aside for a moment all of our contemporary sophistication about the radical separation of facts from values, what more patent fact is there about human beings, perhaps even about living beings generally, than their goal-directed behavior? Indeed, Aristotle's *Nicomachean Ethics* quite unblushingly begins with what in many respects is no more than a truism:

> Every art and every investigation, and likewise every practical pursuit and undertaking, seems to aim at some good: hence it has been well said that the good is that at which all things aim. . . . As there are numerous pursuits and arts and sciences, it follows that their ends are correspondingly numerous: for instance, the end of the science of medicine is health, that of the art of ship building a vessel, that of strategy victory, that of [domestic economy] wealth.[1]

From this, Aristotle moves to the natural conclusion:

> If therefore among the ends at which our actions aim there be one which we wish for its own sake, while we wish others only for the sake of this . . . , it is clear that this one ultimate End must be the Good, and indeed the Supreme Good. Will not then a Knowledge of this Supreme Good be also of great practical importance for the conduct of life? Will it not better enable us to attain what is fitting, like archers having a target to aim at? If this be so, we ought to make an attempt to determine at all events in outline what exactly this Supreme Good is, and of which of the theoretical or practical sciences it is the object.[2]

Now the interesting thing about these passages, for our present purpose, is that in Aristotle's eyes, apparently, nothing is quite so much a fact of nature as what he here presents as goal-directed behavior or activity that aims at some end. Hence to suppose that such things as values, ends, and goals must needs be extrinsic to or outside of nature, or that values are in no sense facts of nature, does seem rather far-fetched. On the contrary, nothing is more natural, or more a part of the world of nature, than a manifold variety of natural changes and tendencies, all of them ordered to their appropriate ends and values.

Or, so long as we are being deliberately unsophisticated and taking things simply as we find them, suppose we choose a rather different example to illustrate the same point. Take, say, an acorn—at once a homely and a hackneyed example, to be sure, but perhaps a very revealing one. May we not say that there is something about an acorn that leads us to connect or associate it in some way with a future oak tree? Surely, this does not seem to commit us to any very imaginative, to say nothing of any very foolhardy or reckless, reasoning. Nothing is more natural than that an acorn should develop into an oak; this is simply a fact of nature; an oak is the natural end of an acorn. If an acorn were to develop into something else, say a tadpole or a skyscraper, we should doubtless say that this was not merely unnatural, but that we had had too much!

All this is not to say that merely because the acorn is thus naturally oriented or ordered to its own proper and characteristic perfection, it must necessarily and inevitably attain that perfection. On the contrary, the acorn may fall on rocky ground and so not mature and develop properly. It may become diseased, so that the young sprout withers and dies. It may even be eaten by a hog. Nor could any of these somewhat untoward events be said to be unnatural. At the same time, so far as the acorn itself is concerned, there is an entirely proper sense in which such happenings may be said to be bad for it, in that they prevent or impede it from attaining its natural perfection or end. And correspondingly, those circumstances and events may be said to be good for it which further its natural growth and development. Indeed, following Aristotle's terminology, the good of the acorn is simply the attainment of its natural end or perfection, the good of anything being that at which it naturally aims—or, since the word "aims" in English usually connotes conscious purpose, we might paraphrase the Aristotelian dictum by saying that the good of anything is simply that toward which it naturally tends or to which it is naturally ordered in its development.

Thus from Aristotle's point of view, it is not necessary to go outside the world of nature in order to discover such things as goods and values. On the contrary, values are simply facts of nature. To find what the good of anything is or what is of value for it, we need not go beyond our ordinary human experience, which suffices to disclose the capabilities and potentialities of things, what their tendencies are, and hence what the ends or goals are toward which they are naturally oriented in their natural growth and development.

Nor is it hard to see how this whole descriptive paraphernalia—potentiality, ends, goals, tendency, natural perfection, natural growth and development, etc.—which might be considered to be originally appropriate to the biological realm, can quite readily and properly be transferred to the human realm. For man is certainly part of the world of nature. Accordingly, just as plants and animals all have natural states of perfection and maturity, toward which their very being is ordered and oriented and in the direction of which they will naturally tend and develop, provided that adverse conditions do not interfere, so also man may be presumed to have his characteristic end or natural perfection, toward which his life naturally tends and at which he aims naturally; this may therefore be called the natural good for man or the human good.

Of course, since a human being is more than just a living organism, it may be presumed that human perfection or the human good will involve something more than mere biological maturity or mere physical health or well-being, as in the case of plants and animals. Rather the human good will involve what might loosely be called the maturity or healthy condition of the whole man, or of man in his total being. Likewise, since man is a being capable of intelligence and understanding, and consequently of planned and deliberate behavior on the basis of such understanding, it may also be presumed that the way in which a human being attains his appropriate good or natural perfection will be rather different from that of a plant or an animal. In the case of the latter, the organism will, as we say, just "naturally" grow and develop to maturity, if unfavorable conditions do not interfere. In contrast, a human being can presumably attain his perfection only by a conscious recognition of what the human end is and by deliberately aiming at this proper end. In this sense, we might say that throughout all the rest of nature, natural perfection is attained "naturally" and through natural processes, whereas in the case of human beings such perfection is attained only by art and design. But in either case the perfection or the good that is so attained is a natural one, being determined by the very nature of the being in question: by the nature of the acorn in the case of the acorn and the oak, and by the nature of man in the case of human beings.

3. What, then, is man's natural end?

Perhaps we can do no better than to let Aristotle present his own account of what this natural end or natural good for a human being is. In his characteristically terse, but illuminating, fashion, he says:

> We may now return to the Good which is the object of our search, and try to find out exactly what it can be. For good appears to be one thing in one pursuit or art and another in another: it is different in medicine from what it is in strategy, and so on with the rest of the arts. What definition of the Good then will hold true in all the arts? Perhaps we may define it as that for the sake of which everything else is done. This applies to something different in each different art—to health in the case of medicine, to victory in that of strategy, to a house in architecture, and to something else in each of the other arts: But in every pursuit or undertaking it describes the end of that pursuit or undertaking, since in all of them it is for the sake of the end that everything else is done. Hence if there be something which is the end of all things done by human action, this will be the practicable Good—or if there be several such ends, the sum of these will be the Good.[3]

Proceeding further, he then asks more directly just what the Supreme Good for man may be considered to be. And his answer is:

> Perhaps then we may arrive at this by ascertaining what is man's function. For the goodness or efficiency of a flute-player or sculptor or craftsman of any sort, and in general of anybody who has some function or business to perform, is thought to reside in that func-

tion; and similarly it may be held that the good of man resides in the function of man, if he has a function.

Are we then to suppose that, while the carpenter and the shoe-maker have definite functions or businesses belonging to them, man as such has none, and is not designed by nature to fulfill any function? Must we not rather assume that just as the eye, the hand, the foot and each of the various members of the body manifestly has a certain function of its own, so a human being also has a certain function over and above all the functions of his particular members? What then precisely can this function be? The mere act of living appears to be shared even by plants, whereas we are looking for the function peculiar to man; we must therefore set aside the vital activity of nutrition and growth. Next in the scale will come some form of sentient life; but this too appears to be shared by horses, oxen, and animals generally. There remains therefore what may be called the practical life of man as possessing reason.[4]

In other words, the good of man, according to Aristotle, turns out to be not simply a matter of staying alive and of performing the vegetative functions that are characteristic of plants. It is not even a matter of merely exercising the ordinary animal functions, which man, of course, has, just like any other animal. Instead, man's natural perfection involves, in addition, the exercise of those powers and capacities that are distinctively human, that is, intelligence and rational understanding. And this brings us right back to Socrates again, for whom the good life for man is simply the examined life, the so-called unexamined life being just not worth living.

4. First objection: this is nothing but a lot of platitudes

Now isn't all this simple and obvious enough? At the same time, unfortunately, it must seem trite enough too. Indeed, so jaded and platitudinous must expressions such as "reason," "intelligence," "natural perfection," "human understanding," "the examined life," appear, that to state one's case in such terms is to risk losing the case forthwith. And yet the fault may lie not with our language but with ourselves, that man's rationality should have become such a commonplace as to lose all significance for actual living men.

Suppose we put to ourselves the following hypothetical case. Suppose someone offers to make a deal with us, be it some dictator, or the Great Leviathan, or the devil himself. He reminds us of how precarious our existence is: We are never free from worries, fears, anxieties, dread, insecurity of all kinds—the atom bomb, economic collapse, political revolution, personal failure, family tragedy. What we are offered, therefore, will be freedom from all this, freedom from fear, freedom from want, freedom from worry. The promise is that we shall be taken care of completely and absolutely—our physical needs, our biological needs, in fact anything that we want. And the price? It will only be that we shan't know what is going on. Oh, we'll be conscious all right, conscious enough to be aware of our desires and of the fact that they are being fulfilled. But we must not expect either to know what is really going on or even to pretend to know. The very pretense or the illusion of "knowing what the score is" will be denied us.

Such is the bargain. Would we accept it? Surely not. It is true that in moods of defeatism, of misery, and of utter hopelessness men have accepted such bargains. Indeed, it might be said that it was in effect just such a bargain that a defeated German people accepted when after the First World War they entrusted their future to Hitler. Still, even though men have entered into such bargains in the past, and even though they will doubtless continue to be tempted by such prospects in the future, by and large no man in his senses would prefer the existence of a contented cow, however well fed and well cared for, to the existence of a human being with at least some understanding of what is going on.

No matter how stupid and ignorant and obtuse a man may be— yes, even if he acknowledges to himself his own intellectual inferiority, taken in the strict and narrow sense—still it is more than likely that what keeps such a person going and makes life bearable for him is his own secret, or perhaps not so secret, conviction that when it comes to his personal decisions and personal choices, he's not really so dumb, and that, according to his lights, he is after all pretty shrewd in the matters of what Aristotle, in the above-quoted passage, termed "the practical life of man as possessing reason."

If not the reality, then at least the pretense or illusion of knowing what it is all about and of what the smart thing to do is—this, we would suggest, means more to a human being than anything else. And this is why, in the hypothetical bargain which we suggested might be offered to a man, we were careful to state the terms in such a way that even the pretense or illusion of knowing would have to be given up in exchange for the promised contentment and security and freedom from want and worry. Indeed, no would-be modern dictator would ever go this far, the technique of dictatorship and demogoguery being rather to make men think they are clever and informed and even wise, while in fact depriving them of the reality of all genuine knowledge and understanding.

In other words, the very exigencies of trying to control people by keeping them in the dark, while making them believe they are in the light, tend to confirm Aristotle's judgment of the supreme value to man of being enlightened, of knowing what is going on—of an intelligent or an examined life, in other words. For whether we be really fools or not, we human beings want at least to believe that we are wise. It is for this reason that Aristotle can quite legitimately say that the supreme good for man is simply to live intelligently.

5. Second objection: what has intelligence got to do with being a good man?

Another difficulty with this Aristotelian dictum is likely to suggest itself at this point. For merely to contrast the intelligent life of man with the vegetative existence of plants or the sensate existence of animals is entirely compatible with pointing to any number of human beings who are certainly intelligent enough, but whose lives we should hardly think of as being examples of human perfection, natural or otherwise. For example, what about Joseph Goebbels or perhaps Joseph Stalin? Certainly, there was no denying them intelligence. What's more, they did not fail to put their intelligence to work in the practical pursuit of their various ends. In this sense, they did not live out their lives on any mere vegetative or sentient level. And yet at the same time, theirs were anything but examined lives in the Socratic sense, for in the case of two such masterminds of national and international ill-will, it is all too obvious that their knowledge was not sought as the source of self-understanding, of knowing oneself. Instead, it was wholly instrumental to ends other than knowledge and understanding, ends such as power, greed, vengeance, and self-aggrandizement. In this sense their lives were not intelligent or examined lives at all.

For that matter, one has but to recall the earlier quoted passage, in which Socrates reproaches his fellow Athenians for being so concerned with heaping up the greatest amount of money and honor and reputation. The chances are that the attainment of these ends will require not merely luck, but no little wit and intelligence—perhaps more indeed than you or I possess, and maybe even more than Socrates or Aristotle possessed. Nor is it likely that Socrates was any more unaware of this simple fact of life than he was of most others. But even though the man whose goal in life is wealth, and whose intelligence happily suffices for attaining it, is likely to be a very shrewd and intelligent fellow, that still does not mean that his life may properly be said to be an intelligent one. For intelligence in his case is presumably used as a mere instrument in the service of ends other than intelligence itself, and that can only be described as foolish and mistaken.

In justification of this latter statement, one has but to examine and reflect upon such an attitude toward life as would make of wealth the be-all and end-all of human existence. It is only too obvious that wealth by its very nature is but a means to other things—to the things that money can buy. This is not to say that such things may not be exceedingly valuable, and passionately coveted, particularly if one doesn't have them; and so too are money and wealth as the means of their purchase. But the point is that means are not ends, and to confuse the former with the latter is but folly and stupidity. Indeed, it takes rather more wisdom and understanding to know how to use riches, once one has them, than it does to know how to acquire them in the first place. That's why there is no fool quite like a rich fool, and also why anyone who uncritically pursues wealth as the principal goal in life, however intelligent he may be, just isn't very smart after all.

Moreover, the same thing may be said of the man whose consuming passion in life is the lust for power. Whatever brilliance and resourcefulness he may display in the pursuit of his end, the end itself is not an intelligent one, being by the very nature of the case a means to something else: power to do this or that or the other. Little wonder, then, that the life of a Goebbels or a Stalin strikes us as being somehow warped, distorted, misspent, and in this sense unnatural: it is not the kind of life that intelligence and understanding would prescribe.

Similarly, to seek honor or reputation as an end is equally unintelligent, however much it may be necessary to exploit one's intelligence in their attainment. To be sure, unlike wealth and power, such things as a good name and a respected position in the community are not necessarily mere means to the attainment of still further ends. Hence they can hardly be criticized for involving an obvious confusion of means with ends. At the same time, suppose we ask ourselves just why we are so anxious about our reputations (for most of us certainly are). One man wants to get ahead in the world and "show the folks back home." Another seeks military glory. Another craves newspaper publicity. Another wants to get to the top of the academic ladder. Another wants to write a book that will head the best-seller lists. Still another wants to be the "man of the year" of the local Rotary Club or Junior Chamber of Commerce. And so on. In fact, in present-day America there seems to be a mania for doing the done thing, whatever profession or walk of life we happen to be in, so that we shall achieve some sort of recognition on the part of our fellows.

But why is this? Why do we seek recognition so avidly? When we think about it a little, we can readily see that we do not, or at least we should not, seek honor and reputation for their own sake, but only because such praise and respect from our fellows somehow serve as reassurance to ourselves that maybe we have accomplished something or amounted to something after all. In other words, honor and reputation are not properly ends at all, but only marks or signs of the end. And what is the end itself? Presumably, it is simply our own worth, our own real achievement and perfection. That is what we are really after; and in so far as we come to think only of our fame and reputation in other men's eyes and not of our own selves and what we ourselves are, to this same extent we are again being no more than foolish and unintelligent: for such an attitude and way of life will not bear scrutiny.

What, then, must such real worth and achievement consist in, a worth and excellence that are to be sought and cherished for their own sake and regardless of whether or not they bring with them fame and reputation and recognition by our fellows? If the whole of our foregoing argument is to be credited, such excellence may be found to lie in the exercise of our characteristic human function, that is to say in leading an intelligent or examined life. Moreover, it should now be clear that such a life must needs be one in which one's knowledge and intelligence are employed, not as mere means for the achievement of irrational ends, but rather as prescribing and determining the ends themselves. This and this alone will constitute a truly intelligent and examined life, and as such will involve that very perfection and fulfillment of one's human nature toward which one is, as we have seen, oriented by nature.

Nevertheless, no sooner do we thus seek to establish the fact that the natural and "healthy," and hence good, life for a human being is simply the life of knowledge and understanding, than another and still more serious misunderstanding is likely to arise. For one might be inclined rather naïvely to suppose that in the present day those whose lives are devoted to the pursuit of such things as "wisdom and truth," as contrasted with "money, honor, and reputation," are none other than the scholar-scientist professors of our great academic institutions. Accordingly, applied to the contemporary scene, it would appear that the good life for man, as Socrates and Aristotle envisage it, would turn out to be none other than the academic life, the life of the professor! With such a denouement, one may well begin to wonder about the wisdom of the Greeks. Such a peripateia might even constitute the *reductio ad absurdum* of Socratic and Aristotelian ethics alike.

Fortunately, though, it is not so much Aristotle who is here at fault, as the somewhat questionable chain of reasoning that carried us blithely from the Socratic ideal of the examined life to the pathetic reality of present-day academic life. For one thing, it takes but little perceptiveness to see that many of our more distinguished exemplars of the academic life today are not exactly men for whom wisdom and truth mean more than money, honor, and reputation. To be sure, money in such cases is probably coveted not so much in the possession of it as in the lack of it. But as for honor and reputation, these are the things that really spur the young academic hopeful to toil endlessly in laboratory or library, grinding out his research, picking up

Guggenheim and Rockefeller grants as he ascends the ladder of academic success, and finally turning out to be an international authority on hormone solutions or the pottery of the Zuni Indians. And as for wisdom and truth, these are not the things that matter academically. No, it's the national or international reputation that counts!

But even should we be more sparing in our satire, and focus attention upon those among our contemporary scholars and scientists—and there are not a few such—for whom a genuine love of knowledge and learning is the dominant motive of their lives, it would still seem that there was a marked discrepancy between the end and purpose of their lives and the idea of the examined life or the intelligent life as represented by Socrates. Indeed, in the preceding chapter, we had a good deal to say about how, in modern science and scholarship, the pursuit of knowledge for its own sake is curiously irrelevant to the development of the scientist's or scholar's own character and personality. That is why we are all too frequently impressed today only with a scientist's brilliance or a scholar's learning, without being the least bit impressed with the man himself as a human being.

Obviously, however, in his praise of the life devoted to wisdom and truth Socrates did not have in mind any such travesty as this. Instead, it is noteworthy that to attain the examined life it is not sufficient that knowledge be sought as an end and not just as a means. In addition, Socrates is always careful to stress that the kind of knowledge and wisdom in which human perfection consists is the knowledge of "Know thyself" and the wisdom that makes for the improvement of the soul.

But imagine a modern economist or medieval historian, to say nothing of a chemist or a nuclear physicist, saying that his whole scientific or scholarly activity was directed simply to the end of a greater self-knowledge and the improvement of his own soul. There is something about nearly all modern science and scholarship that seems to make it not merely impertinent, but actually antithetic to anything on the order of Socratic wisdom.

To be sure, it may not be uncommon for a learned professor, when a testimonial dinner is given in his honor just before his retirement, or when he is invited to speak informally at a luncheon club, to let himself be so carried away by the flattering spirit of the occasion as to expatiate, if he be a mathematician, on the great value of the study of algebra, say, for developing integrity and efficiency of character, or, if he be a folklorist, on how a familiarity with the structure of the folk tale contributes directly to the production of a wise and benign philosophy of life. Given extremely favorable circumstances, one might even hear that there is nothing quite like the close and painstaking study of fossils for developing in a man a really progressive and forward-looking attitude toward human existence.

Yet clearly, all such academic moralizings as vehicles for professorial self-congratulation are more in the nature of professional lapses than they are integral to the actual academic disciplines themselves. Kierkegaard, in his effort to characterize "an existing individual" in contrast to a mere "abstract thinker," puts his finger on the very nerve of Socratic wisdom and by implication sets it off strikingly from the characteristic academic wisdom of the present day:

> An existing individual . . . certainly thinks, but he thinks everything in relation to himself, being infinitely interested in existing. Socrates was thus a man whose energies were devoted to thinking; but he reduced all other knowledge to indifference in that he infinitely accentuated ethical knowledge. This type of knowledge bears a relation to the existing subject who is infinitely interested in existing.[5]

It may have occurred to the reader that in the last few paragraphs it was always to the authority of Socrates that we seemed to be appealing and not to that of Aristotle. Can it truly be said of Aristotle what the foregoing quotation from Kierkegaard so aptly says of Socrates, that it was not knowledge as such that he sought after, so much as self-knowledge; it was not knowledge for its own sake, so much as knowledge for the sake of the enlightenment and direction, which only knowledge can provide, in how to live and how to be human?

The answer to this question is not easy. For in the passage from the *Nicomachean Ethics* which was quoted earlier,[6] we found Aristotle insisting that man's proper function and true end could hardly consist in merely staying alive (even plants can do this) or in performing the characteristic animal functions (horses and oxen can do this). No, the proper life for a human being will be "the practical life of man as possessing reason." Moreover, one can interpret this as meaning that man's true end consists in nothing more than simply living intelligently. And to *live* intelligently is not merely to have a high I.Q., nor is it even to have professorial resources of erudition; rather it is to have such knowledge as is relevant to one's life as a human being, and to bring such humanly relevant knowledge to bear on the conduct of one's own life.

So construed, the words of Aristotle do turn out to be equivalent to Socrates' advocacy of the examined life. But readers of the *Ethics* will remember that in addition to the passage just cited from Book I, there are also those celebrated seventh and eighth chapters of Book X, where Aristotle unequivocally proclaims that the true end of man and the good life for man must needs consist precisely in thought, in intellectual activity, in contemplation (*theōria*) — that is to say, in knowledge for its own sake.* "That happiness consists in contemplation," he says, "may be accepted as agreeing both with the result already reached and with the truth. For contemplation is at once the highest form of activity (since the intellect is the highest thing in us, and the objects with which the intellect deals are the highest things that can be known). . . ."[7]

A few paragraphs further on there occurs that extraordinary passage in which Aristotle seeks to approximate a human life devoted to contemplation to no less than the divine life:

> Such a life as this however will be higher than the human level: not in virtue of his humanity will a man achieve it, but in virtue of something within him that is divine; and by as much as this something is superior to his composite nature, by so much is its activity superior to the other forms of virtue. If then the intellect is something divine in comparison with man, so is the life of the intellect divine in comparison with human life. Nor ought we to obey those who enjoin that a man should have man's thoughts and a mortal

---

*No doubt the pursuit of knowledge for its own sake, as this is manifested in modern scientific and scholarly pursuits, is rather different from the Aristotelian goal of *theōria* or contemplation. But this difference is irrelevant for our present purposes. Suffice it to say that both the modern pursuit of knowledge for its own sake and the Aristotelian goal of contemplation are very different from the Socratic goal of self-knowledge and the examined life, or even, in another context, from Aristotle's own goal of living intelligently.

the thoughts of mortality, but we ought so far as possible to achieve immortality and do all that men may to live in accordance with the highest thing in him; for though this be small in bulk, in power and value it far surpasses all the rest.[8]

Aristotle leaves no doubt that he means to distinguish and exalt such a life of contemplation and thought as against a life devoted merely to bringing one's thought and one's intelligence to bear on one's actions. For "the life of moral virtue," he says, in contrast to the life of mind and of contemplation, "is happy only in a secondary degree. For the moral activities are purely human."[9]

Now just what are we to make of this—that Aristotle changed his views between Book I and Book X, or that he was simply inconsistent, or that the two views are in some subtle fashion reconcilable and compatible after all? Well, as we have remarked before, our concern is not with historical questions as to just what Aristotle did mean or did not mean in this or that passage. Instead, suppose we simply assume Aristotle's own teaching in this connection to be in direct conflict with what we are here contending. Suppose that he did not consider man's true end to consist in *living* intelligently so much as in the exercise of intelligence for its own sake, in the pursuit of knowledge and in the contemplation of truth.

If this was Aristotle's position, then we have no alternative but to "lay hands on our father" Aristotle and to come out in flat disagreement with him on this particular matter. The basis of our disagreement is simply our unshakable conviction that living is not for the sake of knowing, but rather that it is toward intelligent living that all of our powers and capacities are ultimately directed, including our powers of knowledge, and that it is the man himself who counts for more than all his knowledge, no matter how great the latter may be.* In short, knowledge for its own sake can never be the be-all and end-all of human

---

*Needless to say, such a divergence from Aristotle would appear neither arbitrary nor extraordinary, even within an Aristotelian context, the minute one recognizes that the human intellect is an integral part of the human person, and not (as Aristotle himself seems to imply in that cryptic and puzzling passage in the *De Anima*, Book III, Ch. 5) an extraneous and divine element that enters into man, as it were, from the outside.

existence, nor can the chief good of man ever consist in the mere possession or even the exercise of knowledge. Not in the exercise of knowledge as such, but in its use in the practical living of our lives under the guidance of such knowledge and understanding as we possess,* must our characteristic perfection as human beings be thought to consist.

To sum up this rather vexed and crabbed section on the bearing of intelligence on human character, we may say that intelligence as a mere instrument of wealth or power or prestige is not ethically significant. Nor is it intelligence pursued for its own sake that ethics prescribes as the end and goal of our lives. Instead, it is intelligence applied to the problem of living—directed not toward unintelligent ends like wealth or power, but toward making the proper choices in our conduct as men. This is man's true end, or function, or *ergon,* as Aristotle called it. The intelligent man, in this sense, is the good man or the man of character, and, vice versa, the good man, in the sense of the man who has attained his full perfection or natural end as a human being, is the intelligent man.

---

*It is questionable whether going this far need commit one to going quite as far as Kierkegaard represents Socrates as going (cf. the passage cited above, p. 38). For Kierkegaard seems to think that "ethical knowledge" must be such as to involve a kind of thinking in which one thinks "everything in relation to oneself" and that therefore Socrates, while certainly "a man whose energies were devoted to thinking was nevertheless a thinker who reduced all other knowledge to indifference in that he infinitely accentuated ethical knowledge."

However, the retort which Aristotle once made to considerations of this kind still seems altogether just and relevant. In opposition to those who would insist that we confine ourselves simply to a knowledge of man and of the things useful and important to man, Aristotle replied that while "it may be argued that man is superior to the other animals, that makes no difference: since there exist other things far more divine in their nature than man" (1141 a33–b2).

Nevertheless, one can certainly concede the point which Aristotle here makes without thereby being forced to admit that the pursuit of knowledge for its own sake is man's highest activity and ultimate goal. On the contrary, the knowledge of things more important and significant (more "divine") than ourselves, and hence of things worth knowing for their own sake, may be of the utmost significance and relevance to us precisely in our moral behavior and the conduct of our lives.

6. The good life as equivalent to the happy life

And so, however strangely it may strike us, the course of our argument thus far seems to point unmistakably to the conclusion that the good life for a human being is simply the intelligent life, and that the good for man consists in nothing more or less than living intelligently. Nor is that all. For just as the good for a human being may be equated with what is natural for man, in the sense of his natural end or natural perfection, and just as this natural human end or perfection may be seen to amount to no more than a man's living in a characteristically human way—i.e., in his living intelligently—so also we may now note that all of these, man's true good, his natural end or goal, and his living intelligently, may, in turn, be equated with happiness. The good life or the intelligent life, in other words, turns out to be none other than the happy life.

Here, surely, we again join forces with Aristotle—supposing that we did in fact momentarily part company with him. For not the least interesting feature of Aristotle's *Ethics* is the effort which the philosopher makes to give an account of human happiness which would make it not a mere matter of subjective feeling on the part of the individual, but something objectively determinable. To put it in colloquial language, the relevant consideration seems to run something like this: a man might *think* he was in excellent health because he *felt* just fine, yet a medical examination would show that he was far from well; so also a man might think himself to be quite happy and contented, because he would feel quite satisfied and not at all inclined to either complaining or self-reproach, yet it would be only too obvious to an objective observer that this "happy" man was really no better than a fool, his whole way of life being not intelligent, but stupid and unenlightened and perhaps even mean and petty, and so, in a perfectly objective sense, miserable and unhappy.

"But," you may retort, "if a man feels contented and happy and satisfied, is he not really so?" To which the answer is that being satisfied or contented or happy must always involve being satisfied or contented or happy in something or with something or by something. The question then becomes: in what sort of thing does a given individual find satisfaction? If it is in anything less than what as a human being he is capable of and what, as we have already seen, he is naturally ordered and oriented toward, then we should certainly say that such a person had settled for less than he should have, or that he didn't know what was good for him, or that his sense of achievement and satisfaction and therefore of happiness had somehow become perverted and corrupted.

In other words, as Aristotle sees it, the examined life is a goal or end toward which any and every human being is naturally oriented, regardless of whether he knows it or not, and regardless of whether he actually attains it or not, much as an acorn is ordered by nature to its own complete development and perfection as a full-grown oak. Of course, a human being, being a creature of understanding and choice, is to be contrasted with the acorn, in that a man cannot possibly attain to his perfection by any mere process of natural development. Instead, his end can be reached only by art and design. Moreover, what this art of living, which is called ethics, is supposed to teach a man is nothing more nor less than how to live in a characteristically human way, i.e., wisely and intelligently, not being guided by whim or passion, not by mere social convention or external authority, but by the light of truth itself as this illumines his understanding and so serves as a beacon to light the way in his every decision. Nor is it any wonder that if and when a human being does succeed in living in this intelligent and enlightened way, he will be fully aware of his life as being an examined life and hence a life that is proper to man. In other words, it is the life that satisfies man's natural aspirations and strivings and tendencies; and because it is thus satisfying, it is the truly happy life.

Accordingly, whether we call it human perfection or human happiness, human moral goodness or human well-being, it is obvious that, on such a view of ethics, human excellence or virtue will be, in Plato's words, "a kind of health and beauty and good habit of the soul; and vice will be a disease and sickness and deformity of it." Commenting on this passage, Lowes Dickinson once aptly observed: "It follows that it is as natural to seek virtue and to avoid vice as to seek health and avoid disease."[10]

7. A third objection: the evidence from modern science fails to confirm this view of man and of man's natural end

We can no longer try to divert or dam up a mounting wave of objection which must have suggested itself to many readers from the beginning of the present chapter, and which has no doubt gathered an almost irresistible momentum now that our own argument has risen to its climax. You are no doubt saying to yourself that all the full-blown rhetoric at the conclusion of the last section would not have been possible without one simple, but utterly indefensible, assumption, that is, that there is such a thing as a natural end or goal toward which human life and human existence are naturally ordered and oriented. But this will strike you as being nothing but out-and-out teleology, something which was taken for granted in the Aristotelian science of the Middle Ages, but which has been completely displaced by the scientific revolution of the seventeenth century and is now as dead as a doornail.

You may in charity concede a certain superficial plausibility to our arguments in support of the idea of a natural end or natural perfection of human life. But this, you will insist, is only because in our uncritical, everyday reasoning we all constantly fall back upon various and sundry usages and assumptions of common sense and common language. Thus we certainly do, as regards plants and animals and human beings, distinguish between healthy specimens and sickly ones, between those that reach a certain maturity and perfection and those that fail to do so. We also assume—quite uncritically perhaps, but none the less quite regularly—that such distinctions between the healthy and the diseased, the full-grown and the stunted, the good and the bad, are not merely arbitrary and conventional, but have a basis and foundation in nature itself. And from this it is but an easy step, and a step that we all unhesitatingly take in ordinary everyday life, to the assumption of such things as natural ends, natural perfections, natural values, and natural goods.

Still, we have only to draw ourselves up sharp with the stern reminder contained in that one magic word "science," and we shall immediately banish from our minds all unclean thoughts of teleology, of natural goals, and hence of a natural foundation for ethics. No self-respecting modern biologist would ever say any such thing as that the natural good of the acorn is the attainment of its full growth as an oak. He would probably say that so far as the natural order itself is concerned, the full maturity or the healthy condition of a plant is no "better" and no "worse" than for it to be in a dwarfed or diseased condition. In fact, disease is just as natural as health, both alike being the results of equally natural causes. And as for the notion that it can be determined scientifically that it is better and more natural for a man to live intelligently and wisely rather than foolishly and ignorantly—this is so far-fetched as not even to merit a rejoinder.

So once again we are brought face to face with our old and apparently insuperable difficulty: that values can have no possible basis in fact, that no matter how much knowledge we acquire of the facts of nature, we shall never find any evidence there of any distinctions between good and bad, better and worse, right and wrong. Presumably, if ethics is to be justified and established on any sort of a firm basis, it can be only through an appeal to something other than actual facts, or natural happenings and natural processes.

In short, there seems to be no way of defending our basic thesis save by challenging the authority of science itself, and such lese majesty is something for which we would have neither stomach nor wit. Nevertheless, the situation may not be so desperate after all. For without challenging directly the authority of science, it may be possible to show that such authority as science very justly possesses really has no pertinence or bearing in the present instance.

At one time everyone took it for granted that whatever the scientists could find no evidence for didn't exist. But times are different now. It has come to be generally recognized that while the truths of science are unimpeachable in science's own sphere, that sphere is a restricted one. Moreover, its restrictions are imposed by a kind of initial fiat or self-denying ordinance on the part of scientific enterprise itself. We have already had occasion to quote from C. P. Snow's novel *The Search*,[11] where the principal character frankly exposes both the restrictive and the restricted nature of science.

Science was true in its own field; it was perfect within its restrictions. One selected one's data—set one's puzzle for oneself, as it were— and in the end solved the puzzle by showing how they fitted other data of the same kind. We know enough of the process now to see the quality of the results it can give us; we know, too, those sides of experience it can never touch. However much longer science is done, since it sets its own limits before it can begin, those limits must remain.

In virtue of the self-imposed limitations and exclusions of science, the scientific universe will be colorless and tasteless, purposeless and valueless, and perhaps even soulless and mindless. Nor will there be any evidence of teleology in such a universe, and certainly no factual basis for value judgments, to say nothing of moral judgments of any kind.

Given the admittedly restrictive nature of the scientific enterprise, one can scarcely infer from the absence of ends and values in the scientific picture of nature the absence of ends and values in nature absolutely. Even if a program of positivism could be worked out with complete philosophical consistency, the adequacy of such an account of things would still be open to question, not merely in practice but also in principle. For even supposing that no one could produce evidence of any phenomena—of free voluntary action, or final causes, or conscious purposes, or aesthetic values, or extrasensory perception, or whatnot—which the positivist could not account for on his own scientific terms, still the demonstration could be only persuasive and not conclusive, for the reason that the possibility of explanation in scientific terms must involve the exclusion *a priori* of all such data as do not lend themselves to the particular procedures of scientific testing and verification.

Nor is it merely the limited and restricted character of scientific truth that makes it questionable whether it has any particular pertinence or bearing on matters of ethics. There is also the question of whether the scientific universe is something which one can live with practically, however much one may be convinced of its sufficiency theoretically. Indeed, there is in this connection a practical or existential issue in regard to the relevancy and sufficiency of science not unlike the sort of issue that we met with earlier in connection with relativism. Consider for a moment the scientific universe—whether that of microscopic and subatomic physics, where the principle of indeterminacy comes into play, or that of macroscopic physics, where the theory of relativity is operative; how very different this scientific universe is from the world of every day, the world of colors and sounds, of sunrises and sunsets, of birth and death, of "old forgotten far-off things and battles long ago," of winter winds and scorching summers, of bitter animosities and petty ills, of ambitions and defeats, of justices and injustices, of trials and tribulations, of victories and triumphs, of drudgery and vacations, of sickness and health.

But given the manifest differences between the scientific universe and the world of every day, in which world is it that we, as human beings, "live and move and have our being"? True, the question is ambiguous, and yet there is certainly a sense in which no human being can live and act, eat and sleep, succeed or fail, marry or give in marriage, buy or sell, vote or refuse to vote, anywhere save in the everyday world, however much the same man, as a physicist or chemist or biologist, may be intellectually convinced that the scientific universe is the only reality there is. This is why, practically and existentially considered, the fact of scientific knowledge and sophistication seems to impose a kind of double truth upon us, making of so many of us, if not actual schizophrenics, then at least men whose right hands don't always know what their left hands are doing.

In the light of such considerations, making all due allowances for oversimplification and even exaggeration, we can perhaps begin to understand how the mere fact that scientists, in their capacity as scientists, don't seem to come across any value distinctions in the course of their investigations—all this really isn't relevant one way or another to the principles and the foundations of ethics. Whatever may be true of scientists as scientists, as human beings the same scientists are constantly aware of, and constantly acting upon, what they take to be real value distinctions in the world about them. And it is the evidence that we human beings are able to acquire as human beings, and not necessarily the more restricted and highly artificial evidence that we are able to acquire only in our more specialized capacities as physicists or geologists or psychologists, that is requisite for the purposes of ethics and moral philosophy.

Needless to say, to follow such a line of defense in regard to ethics by no means serves to resolve all problems. On the contrary, any appeal to "two truths," though it may serve to show the irrelevance of the findings of modern science to questions of ethics, still leaves us in the utterly unsatisfactory situation philosophically of having to acknowledge that truth is not one, but many. But this is a problem of general philosophical import and hence not one that need bar the way to an investigation of the particular issues of morals and ethics.

Instead, for the time being and during the course of our present study, may we not adopt as our own a program for ethical research and for the investigation of human nature generally that will parallel in some respects at least the program of phenomenological investigation that the distinguished contemporary French philosopher, M. Merleau-Ponty, has characterized so felicitously:

> This first instruction which Husserl gave phenomenology at its beginning—that it be a "descriptive psychology" or a return "to things themselves"—is first of all the disavowal of science. . . .
>
> Everything I know of the world, even through science, I know from a point of view which is mine or through an experience of the world without which the symbols of science would be meaningless. The whole universe of science is built upon the lived world [*le monde vécu*]; and if we wish to conceive science itself with rigour, while exactly appreciating its sense and significance, we must first re-awaken this experience of the world, for science is its second expression. Science does not have and will never have the same kind of being that the perceived world has, for the simple reason that science is a determination or an explanation of that world. . . .
>
> To return to things themselves is to return to this world as it is *before* knowledge and of which knowledge always *speaks,* and with regard to which all scientific determination is abstract, referential and dependent, just as is geography with regard to the landscape where we first learned what a forest is, or a prairie or river.[12]

In other words, for purposes of ethics our concern will be to try to return, in some sense at least, to the things themselves. While for us this will not mean exactly a return to this world as it is "before knowledge," it will at least involve a return to this world as it is before scientific knowledge, and with regard to which we should certainly want to insist that all scientific determination (in the strict modern sense of "scientific") is "abstract, referential and dependent." In any case, it is the everyday world, the concrete world of ordinary human experience, the world that we find ourselves in and that we must continue to live in as human beings, that is of significance for ethics. It is here that ethics must find the evidence for all its principles and the confirmation of all its conclusions.

3

Why Not Regard Morals and Ethics as Simply an Art of Living?

1. Virtue as skill or know-how

At least one statement from the previous chapter must have struck many of you as incredible, if not downright ridiculous: "It is as natural to seek virtue and to avoid vice as to seek health and avoid disease."[1] But if so, you will no doubt be thinking, how does it happen that so many of us seem so little given to following the way of virtue, preferring instead courses that are much more suggestive of "the primrose path."

Before we can answer this question, we must first address ourselves to the prior question of just what this thing called "virtue" is anyway. What do we mean by such a notion?

In our first chapter we toyed with the idea that living well, or making the most of one's life, was perhaps no more than a matter of art or skill, a matter of knowing how, in other words. Why not, then, simply identify virtue, moral virtue that is to say, with knowing how to live? The virtuous man would then be the man who had acquired the requisite skill in living, or in being human, just as the man who lacked virtue would be the one who hadn't learned how to live, who didn't know what to do or how to do it, and who consequently was well on the way toward making a mess of his life and a fool of himself.

2. *Human feelings, affections, and emotions as that with respect to which the human virtues are exercised*

All well and good. Suppose, therefore, that for the time being we accept the proposal that human virtue be understood as simply the skill or know-how that is appropriate to the business of living. Nevertheless, a skill must always be exercised with respect to some typical kind of situation; likewise, any sort of know-how involves knowing how to do a particular kind of job when faced with a particular kind of problem or situation. Thus a skilled pilot must know how to get his ship through stormy seas, a skilled physician must know how to bring his patient back to health amid conditions of bodily disease and decay, and a skilled investor must know how to conserve and increase his original stake in the face of the fluctuations of the market and of changing business conditions.

What is it, then, that the virtuous man must do? With respect to what sort of situations and problems is his skill exercised? To answer this question suppose we raise a closely related question: In just what sort of situation are we inclined to say that a person has not acted or behaved very intelligently or wisely? The answer is not hard to find. Let anyone ask himself whether he has ever lost his temper, or gotten excited, or been depressed, or felt hurried and pressed for time; and whether under such circumstances he has not at least sometimes done things which he later regretted, things which, as he might say, he should have realized were foolish and unwise, had he not been so angry or so excited or so upset.

Could we say, then, that moral virtue is simply the sort of skill or know-how that enables us to act intelligently — this time not in the face of rough seas or adverse business conditions, but in the face of our own feelings and impulses and emotions? This seems plausible on the face of it. Nevertheless, we need to push the analysis further and consider rather more complicated cases than those of merely getting angry or excited or rattled.

For instance, consider Dryden's satirical portrait of the Earl of Shaftesbury:

Of these the false Achitophel was first;
A name to all succeeding ages curst:
For close designs and crooked counsels fit,
Sagacious, bold, and turbulent of wit,
Restless, unfix'd in principles and place,
In pow'r unpleas'd, impatient of disgrace;
A firey soul, which, working out its way,
Fretted the pigmy body to decay:
And o'er-inform'd the tenement of clay.
A daring pilot in extremity;
Pleas'd with the danger, when the waves went high,
He sought the storms; but, for a calm unfit,
Would steer too nigh the sands, to boast his wit.
Great wits are sure to madness near allied,
And thin partitions do their bounds divide;
Else why should he, with wealth and honor blest,
Refuse his age the needful hours of rest?
Punish a body which he could not please,
Bankrupt of life, yet prodigal of ease?
And all to leave what with his toil he won,
To that unfeather'd two-legg'd thing, a son:
Got, while his soul did huddled notions try;
And born a shapeless lump, like anarchy.
In friendship false, implacable in hate,
Resolv'd to ruin or to rule the State. . . .[2]

Without concerning ourselves with the justice or historical accuracy of this characterization, do we not readily recognize the sorts of "mistakes" and "errors" that a person such as Shaftesbury might be said to have fallen into? His restlessness of spirit, his feelings of bitterness and resentment, his recklessness, his vindictiveness—all these qualities indicate not just passing impulses and momentary feelings that cause a man to do things which even he himself would acknowledge were stupid and foolish. What are involved here are settled habits and patterns of behavior that seem to have rendered the man relatively impervious to saner and more rational counsels. Thus while Shaftesbury himself might not recognize that the way he was conducting himself and what he was making of himself were unwise, we and others who might be in a position to view the situation more objectively can see that this was precisely what was happening.

But does not this only confirm our earlier suggestion that in the business of living what the requisite art or skill must deal with are such things as our own personal inclinations and tendencies, our passions and feelings? It is in the face of these that we must act intelligently, if our concern be to live skillfully and intelligently and not simply to invest money or pilot a plane or try a case skillfully and intelligently.

Let us, though, consider another example, this time one that is admittedly fictional, but one that anyone who has been connected with academic life must recognize as true. It is C. P. Snow's description of one of the characters in *The Masters:*

> I looked round his sitting-room. It was without feature, it was the room of a man concentrated into himself, so that he had nothing to spend outside; it showed nothing of the rich, solid comfort which Brown had given to his, or the eccentric picturesqueness of Roy Calvert's. Nightingale was a man drawn into himself. Suspicion and envy lived in him. They always would have done, however life had treated him; they were part of his nature. But he had been unlucky, he had been frustrated in his most cherished hope and now envy never left him alone.
>
> He was forty-three, and a bachelor. Why he had not married I did not know: there was nothing unmasculine about him. That was not, however, his abiding disappointment. He had once possessed great promise. He had known what it was to hold creative dreams; and they had not come off. That was his bitterness. As a very young man he had shown a spark of real talent. He was one of the earliest theoretical chemists. By twenty-three he had written two good papers on molecular structure. He had, so I was told, anticipated Heitler-London and the orbital theory; he was ten years ahead of his time. The college had elected him, everything seemed easy. But the spark burnt out. The years passed. Often he had new conceptions; but the power to execute them had escaped from him.
>
> It would have been bitter to the most generous heart. In Nightingale's, it made him fester with envy. He longed in compensation

for every job within reach, in reason and out of reason. It was morbid that he should have fancied his chances of the tutorship before Brown, his senior and a man made for the job; but it rankled in him after a dozen years. Each job in the college for which he was passed over, he saw with intense suspicion as a sign of the conspiracy directed against him.

His reputation in his subject was already gone. He would not get into the Royal Society now. But, as March came round each year, he waited for the announcement of the Royal elections in expectation, in anguish, in bitter suspiciousness, at moments in the knowledge of what he might have been.[3]

This passage requires little comment. A man's feelings of envy, of frustration, of suspicion, can prevent him from achieving anything like an examined life in Socrates' sense or an intelligent life in Aristotle's. Again, the sort of situation with respect to which skill in the art of living becomes pertinent is a situation calling for the exercise of intelligence with reference to our own feelings and emotions.

Perhaps one final example may not be out of place in this connection. This time we turn to Miss C. V. Wedgwood's characterization of Charles I:

The small, fastidious King presided fittingly over his well-ordered Court. By nature reserved, he was isolated still more by that slight impediment of the speech which made him shun all but formal contacts, except with his familiars. Even his friends he kept at their distance, but with a regular and courteous demeanour that all understood and some, who were formal themselves, grew to like. . . . The unseemly, the ludicrous, the merely human were excluded from his public life, and almost all his life was public.[4]

The King had a high sense of duty towards the people whom he regarded as a sacred trust from God, but this was compatible with an open dislike of their proximity and their opinions. It was only, perhaps, when he touched for the King's Evil at Easter and Michaelmas that he allowed the vulgar to approach closely to his royal person. . . .

He had never had the painful experience from which his father, as a young man, had learnt so much; he had never confronted insolent opponents face to face and had the worst of the argument. No national danger had compelled him to go out among his people and share their perils. He was, at this time, not only the most formal but the most remote and sheltered of all European kings.

What he knew of men, he knew chiefly by report and study. Like many shy, meticulous men, he was fond of aphorisms, and would write in the margins of books, in a delicate, beautiful, deliberate script, such maxims as "Few great talkers are good doers" or "None but cowards are cruel." He trusted more to such distilled and bottled essence of other men's wisdom than to his own experience, which was, in truth, limited; his daily contact with the world was confined within the artificial circle of his Court and the hunting field.[5]

The ideal was constantly before his eyes but the intellectual and aesthetic fashion of the day, strongly bent towards allegory, obscured the practical difficulties of the task. The King lived in a world of poetic illusions and could not but be affected by them. For him and his courtiers, the most ordinary events were swiftly wreathed in pastoral or classical disguise. The Countess of Anglesey gave an evening party for the Queen and at once the poets summoned the goddess Diana and bade the stars shoot from their spheres. . . .

The allegorical trick in poetry and compliment insensibly spreads to other things and becomes almost a habit of mind. The King seemed sometimes to treat administration and politics as though the peace and contentment of the realm were indeed assured because, at his Christmas revels, a golden chariot upon a white cloud had descended against the heavenly backcloth bearing Peace, "in a flowery vesture like the Spring," with buskins of green taffeta, a garland of olives on her head and a branch of palm in her hand.[6]

Alas, poor Charles, if this account is to be credited. The King's fastidiousness, his timidity, his lethargy in regard to matters of business and public affairs, his aesthetic sensitivity led him to mistake a grandiose baroque dream-world for the harsher world of reality. Little wonder that he should have missed so completely the Socratic objective of knowing himself and, correlatively, knowing the actual human situation in which he found himself. Once again, it becomes clear that living intelligently involves seeing things as they are and seeing oneself as one is, amid all the confusions and misrepresentations due to one's own passions and predilections and prejudices.

3. But what are "feelings," "affections," "emotions," "inclinations"?

What is the nature of these disturbing and seemingly irrational factors in men's behavior which we have rather loosely and indiscriminately labeled "passions," "impulses," "feelings," "emotions," etc.? Apparently, human virtue amounts to no more than a certain skill or competence in dealing with these irrational human affections. But have we any very clear idea of what these things are?

In meeting this challenge we propose not to have recourse to the theories and findings of modern psychology—"When ignorance is bliss, 'tis folly to be wise"—but rather to follow as closely as possible our common human experience in such matters. At the very outset our enterprise would appear to be rendered almost hopeless by virtue of the seemingly limitless diversity and heterogeneity of such things as feelings, desires, emotions, moods, attitudes, and passions. How will it ever be possible to bring these all under a single genus, so that they can all be equally understood as just so many sources of confusion and interference, with respect to the rational conduct of life?

For example, must it not be acknowledged that your feeling of drowsiness and ennui as you read a dull book is a very different thing from Othello's blind and all-consuming passion of jealousy? Do perennial laziness and habits of procrastination have anything in common with that irascible overconfidence and hard self-assurance which belonged to Sophocles' Oedipus? Yet we seem to be suggesting that all of these things—boredom and laziness, Othello's jealousy and Oedipus' self-assurance and even hubris—all of these are to be accounted as strictly comparable factors, in that all alike tend to militate against a really intelligent conduct of life: they blind us to the truth about ourselves and keep us from acting in ways that even our own better judgment would prescribe.

And even if the manifold diversity of human impulses and affections can all be subsumed under one heading, is it not a patent mistake to suppose that all such passions and motives, all such likes and dislikes, are necessarily bad, that they are all recalcitrant and even contrary to the dictates of reason and intelligence? Boredom with a dull book may be a sign of good judgment, and indignation can often be righteous.

In the light of considerations and warnings such as these, our task is now to give such an account of human affections and emotions that not only their generic unity can be made apparent, but also their characteristic ambivalence and ambiguity: whether they are beneficial or harmful, contributory or inhibitory, with respect to our human concern with living intelligently and leading an examined life. Perhaps, though, the task may not be so difficult as it sounds. For one has only to consider the condition, at once so obvious and so universal, in which every human being inevitably finds himself, of being thrown into an environing world of people and things and forced constantly to reckon with what may be advantageous or harmful, pleasant or painful, fortunate or unfortunate, beneficial or disastrous. Under such circumstances, it is not surprising that human beings should have developed various devices of warning and control, thermostats, if you will, which register the approach both of dangers and of benefits, and which then set off the appropriate reactions and dispositions on the part of the organism—say, fear in the case of threatened harm, or desire in the case of a promised benefit, or despair in the case of seemingly certain disaster.

4. A possible classification of desires and emotions according to their respective thermostatic functions

In this connection, some of the more old-fashioned schemes for classifying the passions and emotions are by no means uninstructive. For instance, one mode of classification[7] was to consider the feelings of so-called love and hate as basic. By "love" and "hate" were meant no more than approval or liking for what appears to be good or beneficial, and disapproval or dislike for what is taken to be evil or harmful. The English words "love" and "hate" are really too strong and too heavily charged to convey properly the relatively neutral and general idea of an opposition between what some recent thinkers have called "pro-attitudes" on the one hand, and "con-attitudes" on the other.[8]

In any case one can readily understand how, taking as basic such a pro-attitude toward that which appears to be of worth or value, this attitude becomes desire, when the object of value is absent, and joy or pleasure when it is present. Correspondingly, an attitude of dislike or disapproval, a "con-attitude," becomes a positive aversion when what is disliked is absent and a feeling of pain or distress when it is present. In similar fashion, a feeling or emotion such as fear is to be understood as the sort of response that is appropriate to that which one dislikes, but which instead of being actually present is imminent and threatening. In like manner, various other feelings such as hope, despair, envy, resentment, and anger can be understood in terms of the difficult or easy accessibility or evitability of objects toward which we evince either pro- or con-attitudes.

5. The limitations of these thermostatic controls of our actions and reactions, and the role of the virtues in making up for these limitations

Granting the limitations and inadequacies of such a classificatory scheme for human feelings and emotions, we can nevertheless begin to see, in terms of such a scheme, just what the peculiar nature of man's ethical or moral problem tends to be. It is well and good that our human thermostatic controls should tend to make us fearful in the presence of danger, or eager and desirous in anticipation of what promises to be beneficial, or contented and satisfied on the achievement of something valuable and worth while. But if what we are afraid of should prove to be not a real danger at all, or if what we are so eager to get should in fact not be really valuable, or if what we take to be a cause of self-congratulation and self-satisfaction should actually be something trifling and insignificant, we shall be made to appear foolish and ridiculous.

In other words, there is nothing wrong about a man being angry or pleased or bored or afraid or discouraged or satisfied, provided that the object of his feeling or emotion be truly provoking or pleasing or dull or dangerous or discouraging or satisfying. For without emotions and passions, a human being would not be human, but a mere clod, lacking the dynamic quality that is requisite for the attainment of human perfection. In this sense, then, the common feature that may be said to characterize all of our amazingly diverse and heterogeneous human emotions is not that they tend to be a refractory element, likely to disturb the sane and intelligent conduct of life. On the contrary, our emotions are the very motive, or emotive, forces of our being, moving us toward what we need and what would be of benefit to us, and away from what would be harmful and dangerous and evil.

In this light, then, it becomes clear that all of our human affections and inclinations can be brought under a single heading, as regards their relevance and significance for a truly human life. And it becomes clear also that such appetites and emotions, so far from being all bad, are indispensable aids to, and even promoters of, the good life. Just as the sea is not a hindrance to the skilled pilot, or the national economy an obstruction to the skilled stockbroker, so a man's feelings and emotions are in no wise to be regarded as evil, provided only that the man have the requisite skill in utilizing and handling them. Indeed, in any art or skill, the objective is not to eliminate the material upon which the artist works, but to use and control and become the master of these materials. And so it is in the art of living: the virtuous man is the man who knows how to utilize and control his own emotions and desires.

More specifically, then, on this view morals and ethics are to be regarded as involving no more than learning and knowing how to bring our intelligence and understanding to bear upon our passions and desires. For, as is only too obvious, these latter, in their role of thermostatic controls governing the release of our appetitive and repulsive energies, are none too reliable. Indeed, as should by now be apparent, there is no human pro-attitude or con-attitude, no human emotion or passion or feeling, that does not involve at least an implicit value judgment about something's being good or bad for the individual concerned. But such sub- or pre-rational judgments are frequently misleading. Accordingly, the function of our human reason and intelligence, in a moral context, is to provide a needed corrective to the oft-mistaken judgments implicit in so many of our emotions, as, for example, when we become angry when there is nothing really to be angry about, or when we set our hearts on getting something which is scarcely worth getting excited about, or when we become depressed and feel sorry for ourselves, even though our situation be nothing like as bad as we may have led ourselves to believe.

6. A possible illustration of how these virtues sometimes work: Aristotle's doctrine of the mean

By way of illustration of how such skill or know-how in the business of living tends to operate with respect to our impulses and feelings, it may be instructive to consider briefly Aristotle's celebrated doctrine of the mean. To be sure, this principle may not have the universal applicability in regard to moral questions that Aristotle seemed to think it had. For it seems hardly plausible to assume that in regard to any and every pro- or con-attitude that we may have, the role of intelligent judgment will always and necessarily be one of mediating between excess and defect, as if every such attitude, whether pro- or con-, were bound to be either too much so or too little so. On the other hand, if we accept the assumption, it turns out to be a mere truism which doesn't tell us very much. For how is one helped in the living of one's life merely to be told that one must be careful not to feel too strongly and yet equally careful to feel strongly enough, not to desire a thing too much and yet to desire it enough?

Nevertheless, for all the shortcomings and even dangers of this doctrine of the mean, it may, perhaps, be used as a device for illustrating how something on the order of skill and know-how can be brought to bear on our human likes and dislikes.

To begin with, consider the ordinary run of human responses and feelings with respect to typical situations in which men find themselves —confidence and discouragement, enthusiasm and indifference, cautiousness and carelessness, appreciativeness and scornfulness, friendliness and hostility, worry and unconcern, dissatisfaction and complacency. Now there is no doubt that some of us all of the time, and perhaps most of us some of the time, allow ourselves to worry overmuch about our affairs, or else not to worry enough; to be excessively dissatisfied with our lot, or else lazy and complacent; to be friendly and a hail-fellow-well-met toward everybody, or else churlish and disagreeable; to be ridiculously cautious and careful, or else reckless and by no means careful enough; to be blinded to everything of worth and value except what is dictated by an all-consuming ambition, or else shiftless and lethargic with no get-up-and-get at all; to be the eternal optimist, indiscriminately sanguine about everything, or else the gloomy pessimist with no sure judgment about even those chances and opportunities that are genuine. Nor is there any doubt that the more sensible behavior would be one which managed to observe the just mean between such extremes.

It is true that in such judgments there is a great deal that is relative to the particular situation or that derives from mere social convention. An English gentleman of the nineteenth century was expected to observe a haughtiness and reserve which would have been scarcely appropriate, and even ridiculous, in an Italian fruit peddler of the same period; a trust officer in a bank is expected to display a caution that would hardly be fitting in a wildcat oil operator. And yet, the whole point of the doctrine of the mean is that in the very nature of the case it will be related to the particular situation, the principle being that how we feel and react to a situation should not be a mere uncritical and undisciplined response, but rather the sensible and intelligent reaction which the particular situation calls for. Even though social convention and the traditions in which we have been brought up may color our judgments as to which reactions are excessive and which deficient, the very purpose of the doctrine of the mean is that, by having regard for it, we shall eventually learn to let our judgment as to what is really the mean between two extremes be determined by our intelligence and understanding rather than by mere social convention.

7. A still more specific illustration; the virtue of self-respect and a just sense of dignity and personal responsibility

In order more fully to bring out the import of this doctrine of the mean, considered as a device for determining what our proper feelings and emotions should be on different occasions, we might consider that sort of attitude or feeling toward ourselves which we today would call self-respect or a sense of personal dignity. Indeed, if we are not mistaken, it was somewhat the same sort of attitude that Aristotle sought to designate and describe—not very felicitously perhaps—under the title of magnanimity (*megalopsychia*) or greatness of soul.[9] One might say that a proper respect for and estimate of oneself is not just one virtue among others, but is almost the key to the entire ethical problem. For if Socratic self-knowledge be the essence of the good life, then the man who manages to live well will be the man who has a just estimate of himself, being neither overly complacent about his capacities and achievements, nor, at the other extreme, overly lacking in a sense of his own dignity and responsibilities. Or, to paraphrase one of Aristotle's blunter formulations of the principle: a proper self-respect is nothing but a mean between the two extremes of thinking too much of yourself and thinking too little of yourself.

That most of us are inclined to err on the side of thinking too much of ourselves goes almost without saying. For complacency and smugness, to say nothing of downright vanity, are traits from which we human beings seem to be singularly unsuccessful in freeing ourselves. To take but one example, this time from Jane Austen:

> Sir Walter Elliott of Kellynch Hall, in Somersetshire, was a man who, for his own amusement, never took up any book but the Baronetage; there he found occupation for an idle hour and consolation in a distressed one. . . .
>
> Vanity was the beginning and end of Sir Walter Elliott's character: vanity of person and of situation. He had been remarkably handsome in his youth, and at fifty-four was still a very fine man. Few women could think more of their personal appearance than he did, nor could the valet of any new made lord be more delighted with the place he held in society. He considered the blessings of beauty as inferior only to the blessing of a baronetcy; and the Sir Walter Elliott who united these gifts, was the constant object of his warmest respect and devotion.[10]

Substitute for a baronetcy a Harvard professorship, or a record as a star athlete, or the presidency of the local Lions Club, or a widespread reputation as a lady-killer, or perhaps even first place in a beauty contest, and one will find Sir Walter's vanity paralleled by thousands of American businessmen, professors, athletes, and beauty queens. While few Americans are likely to find "occupation for an idle hour and consolation in a distressed one" in the "Baronetage" they can find ample substitutes in such things as golf trophies, *Who's Who in America,* citations by the local Junior Chamber of Commerce, or maybe even in boxes of colored slides that chronicle in depressing detail their honors, their triumphs, and their travels.

Vanity or smugness, we would all agree, is an extreme variation on the feeling of self-satisfaction, and hence foolish and ridiculous; but is it equally clear that at the other extreme there is such a thing as thinking too little of oneself, which in its own way is just as foolish? At first glance, this does not seem plausible; we naturally assume that if vanity is a fault, then its opposite, modesty or humility, must be a virtue.

We must proceed cautiously here, for while modesty is certainly not a fault—provided it is not mere mock modesty, but a genuine attitude based on accurate self-knowledge and self-appraisal—still it may be questioned whether modesty is, after all, the proper opposite of vanity and complacency. Remember, the basic feeling or attitude that we are here concerned with is one of self-respect, a feeling of one's own worth and dignity. Accordingly, if one extreme consists in overestimating one's own worth, the other extreme is not modesty or humility, but rather what might be called a lack of proper self-respect or an insufficient sense of personal dignity. It is hard to express in one word the quality I am trying to describe—perhaps "self-depreciation" is close enough to suggest the meaning. That this can be a serious and even a frightening thing is brought out in the following quotation from Erich Fromm:

> The modern market is no longer a meeting place but a mechanism characterized by abstract and impersonal demand. One produces for this market, not for a known circle of customers; its verdict is based on laws of supply and demand; and it determines whether the commodity can be sold and at what price. No matter what the use value of a pair of shoes may be, for instance, if the supply is greater than the demand, some shoes will be sentenced to economic death. . . .

. . . the regulatory function of the market has been, and still is, predominant enough to have a profound influence on the character formation of the urban middle class and, through the latter's social and cultural influence, on the whole population. The market concept of value, the emphasis on exchange value rather than on use value, had led to a similar concept of value with regard to people and particularly to oneself. . . .

In our time the market orientation has been growing rapidly, together with the development of a new market that is a phenomenon of the last decades—the "personality market." Clerks and salesmen, business executives and doctors, lawyers and artists . . . all are dependent for their material success on a personal acceptance by those who need their services or who employ them.

The principle of evaluation is the same on both the personality and the commodity market: on the one, personalities are offered for sale; on the other, commodities. . . . only in exceptional cases is success predominantly the result of skill and of certain other human qualities like honesty, decency, and integrity. . . . Success depends largely on how well a person sells himself on the market, how well he gets his personality across, how nice a "package" he is. . . .

The fact that in order to have success it is not sufficient to have the skill and equipment for performing a given task but that one must be able to "put across" one's personality in competition with others shapes the attitude toward oneself . . . since success depends largely on how one sells one's personality, one experiences oneself as a commodity or rather simultaneously as the seller and the commodity to be sold. . . . [one's] self-esteem depends on conditions beyond his control. If he is "successful," he is valuable; if he is not, he is worthless. The degree of insecurity which results from this orientation can hardly be overestimated. . . . Hence one is driven to strive relentlessly for success, and any setback is a severe threat to one's self-esteem; helplessness, insecurity, and inferiority feelings are the result. If the vicissitudes of the market are the judges of one's value, the sense of dignity and pride is destroyed. . . .[11]

From such a description we can discern more clearly the sort of thing involved in this feeling or attitude that we have called self-depreciation, or lack of self-respect. It is the sort of feeling that makes a man willing to sell his soul to the devil, and sometimes very cheaply too—whether the devil is a Hitler who promises such things as national glory and honor, to say nothing of food and employment, at the price of giving up one's critical intelligence and one's responsibility to think for oneself; or whether it is the American "personality market," as Fromm calls it, where one is promised such things as glamour and success if only one will conform, forgoing anything like the examined life and devoting all one's efforts to making oneself a merely saleable or marketable article.

Nor is this the only manifestation of the sort of feeling that we have called lack of self-respect. There are other examples as well, perhaps some that are to be found even closer to home. Suppose you ask yourself: Do you actually believe in such things as personal dignity and personal integrity? Is not all this talk about perfecting oneself as a human being, or recognizing one's capacities and responsibilities, or how only the examined life is worth living—does not all this sound like stuff and nonsense? Can you imagine a character such as Jake, say, in *The Sun Also Rises* talking this way? Or if this be too high-brow, what about Steve Canyon in the comic strips, or Peter Gunn on television? Here are steel-eyed, steel-nerved men, sophisticated, thoroughly disenchanted, taking their pleasures where they find them, and living from day to day, never bothering their heads about the Socratic ideal or any other ideal for that matter, and on the whole simply fancying that the business of living amounts to little more than making the most of life's emptiness and purposelessness.

In other words, this time what we have chosen to call a deficient sense of one's dignity and responsibility as a human being leads not to selling one's soul to the devil, or even to selling one's human birthright for any of the currently popular messes of pottage, but rather in just not selling or buying anything. For nothing seems to be worth anything. You don't amount to anything yourself, and even if you tried to sell yourself, what could you buy with the proceeds that would be any more than a snare and a delusion? Oh, you keep on living, of course, but mainly by diverting yourself—with bullfights, with love affairs, with sports, perhaps even with your job, if you are good at it and it happens to be sufficiently varied and diverting. But basically, living is pretty much a matter of forgetting and being distracted, almost as if you were moving in a dream, performing inane and pointless and often even frustrating activities — but what does it matter, since all of your comings and goings, your doings and undoings, are so wholly without significance as to be almost without reality?

One has but to bring to mind attitudes and feelings of this sort, feelings which reflect not despair so much as just not giving a damn, and one readily recognizes that as compared with feeling overly complacent and satisfied, there is an opposite extreme in which one's life comes to be blighted and distorted from boredom with one's very existence, or perhaps from a kind of sneering and superior indifference to the possibilities and responsibilities of life, or from a cynical conviction of the inanity and pointlessness of human existence.

It is not without irony that in the present day in our own country such attitudes of indifference or even of disgust for the purposes and responsibilities of life have tended to become a source of no little pride and self-satisfaction to many of our contemporaries. An attitude that was originally supposed to be one of stark realism has lately come to deck itself out as an eminently fashionable and hence alluring ideal. How many of us consciously or unconsciously would not like to imagine ourselves as exemplifying in our lives the type of the sophisticated newspaper reporter, or the cool "private eye," or the clear-eyed, no-nonsense "realist"? Certainly, among so-called intellectuals and people in academic life, you have often but to scratch the surface of professional respectability to discover that your man of learning secretly delights in picturing himself as a sort of composite Ernest Hemingway, Jean-Paul Sartre, and perhaps Pablo Picasso.

The result is likely to be not a Hemingway or a Sartre or a Picasso, but only a Sir Walter Elliott. But however amusing or even ridiculous its results may be, there is no denying the fact that what is here being enacted is a curious transvaluation of values, one extreme having been literally transvalued into its opposite. What in its inception was an outlook of little more than hopelessness, desperation, and cynicism in the face of one's human existence tends to take on the character of an ideal worthy of emulation. It has joined the ranks of all those other human poses and postures which are sources of satisfaction and self-congratulation to those who strike them, for they seem to provide us with a sort of reassurance that we are, after all, thank God, not as other men are.

This capacity that men seem to have of managing to pass, almost phoenix-like, from thinking too little of themselves to thinking too much of themselves is likewise exemplified, and perhaps even with greater frequency, among that other group of those whom we have characterized as being deficient in self-respect and a sense of their own worth, those who are all too ready to sell themselves—whether cheaply or for a high price, and whether on the personality market, or to a dictator, or to ordinary purveyors of conformity who flourish in every community. For it is the very person who thinks so little of himself as to be ready to forgo such things as freedom and independence of judgment, to accept the standards of the community uncritically, to do only the done thing—it is he, who having been a success in his conformity, is most likely to become the stuffed shirt, the pompous ass, the unshakable pharisee. Ironically enough, it is such a person's very self-importance which betokens his underlying inclination toward *micropsychia*, thinking too little of himself: he has become satisfied with himself when there is still not much to be satisfied about and when he should be demanding so much more of himself.

But enough by way of examples and illustrations. They may suffice to show how, in many cases, the voice of intelligence in human conduct calls for striking a mean between certain extremes of excess or defect into which we human beings may easily be led, if we uncritically follow the lead of our various feelings, inclinations, and passions. Even more fundamentally, may not such examples serve to show the pertinence of knowledge and understanding to the conduct of life, with the result that living well, or being a success, or making the most of one's life are to be regarded as being pretty much a matter of acquiring and exercising the requisite skill and know-how in what we have chosen to call the art of living?

4

Why Morals and Ethics Are Not Simply an Art of Living

1. Is ethics really an art?

The preceding chapter ended with a question, which was, in effect, whether ethics or morals could be regarded as simply an art of living. Those who remember Plato's Dialogues will recognize that such was the way Plato rather consistently chose to regard ethics. And yet Aristotle, despite his insistence that in ethics one is concerned with learning how to live intelligently, seems to make an abrupt about-face, declaring flatly that morals or ethics, while seemingly no more than an art, is actually different from all the other arts: "In the arts, again, a deliberate mistake is not so bad as an undesigned one, whereas in matters to which practical wisdom is applicable [i.e., in moral or ethical matters], it is the other way round."[1]

Even without the authority of Aristotle and without for the moment bothering one's head over just what is meant by Aristotle's words, it is not hard, simply on one's own, to think of any number of objections to the idea that leading a good life is only a matter of learning how to strike a mean between the extremes of excess and defect, as if ethics were simply an art or a skill. If it were, such an art of living would involve actually learning rules about such things as when to get angry, and when not, and to what degree; or what we may properly become enthusiastic over and what not; or when we may legitimately feel proud of ourselves and when not; or whether one is ever warranted in feeling resentful or envious, and if so, when and under what circumstances.

To this you may well be inclined to make an emphatic rejoinder: "There is no such art. Indeed, it is fatuous to suppose that anyone can ever acquire *knowledge* of things of this sort. In ordinary conversation, perhaps, we may speak of knowing when to be indignant and when not. But surely this is only a manner of speaking, for in the literal sense no one can ever *learn* how to feel or how to respond to a situation, in the way in which a surgeon, for example, learns when and how to perform an appendectomy. Indeed, if one persisted in using the word "knowledge" in both contexts, it would be clear that the term had become ambiguous. For it is only in the latter context that one can be said to have knowledge in the proper sense of a skill, or an art, or know-how. If the art of living consists in nothing more or less than learning how to feel and react toward persons and things, then there is no art of living, and the claim that ethics is a science and constitutes a legitimate body of knowledge is so much stuff and nonsense. Would anyone in his senses claim that by mastering this so-called art of living a young man or woman will thereby learn just when and with whom he or she should fall in love? Or to take another example, can we suppose that when a man is struck a sharp blow on the jaw, his Socratic self-knowledge will instruct him whether or not he should feel angry, or even, presumably, whether or not he should feel pain?"

2. The uncertainty of ethics as comparable to the uncertainty in any art: art deals with the particular and individual

Perhaps, though, the edge of this sort of criticism may be dulled somewhat if we recognize that an art or skill in living is not of the same nature as the highly technical skill of the modern engineer or expert on atomic energy. A more apt comparison might be with a chef's skill in knowing how much seasoning to add to a lamb stew, neither too much nor too little, or with a good driver's skill in knowing just when and how much to brake his car on a dangerous curve, or a musician's skill in his choice of tempo in the rendering of a certain sonata.

Our present knowledge of human passions and affections is too rudimentary and inexact to provide anything like the elaborate and detailed scientific foundation that underlies such present-day skills as electronics, metallurgy, agronomy, and medicine. But more fundamentally, in criticizing the notion of morals or ethics as an art, we often forget what is distinctive of all arts and skills, even the most complex and those resting on the most sophisticated scientific foundations, which is that no skill is ever properly exercised by mechanically following certain rules or by simply going by the book. The reason is that the particular concrete situations which are the actual points of application of any art or skill are always so complex and intricate that no set of general rules and principles ever suffices to cover them completely.

We do not, for example, consider that a surgeon is not skilled merely because he cannot draw up a set of instructions so complete and detailed that all one need do is to follow them automatically and the success of a certain type of operation will thereby be guaranteed. On the contrary, each particular case being different from every other, no one will ever be a skilled surgeon merely by following rules, or by applying a technique automatically. Instead, true skill must involve the adaptation of a technique to the immediate and particular circumstances at hand. For this reason, to master an art—be it that of surgery or carpentry, plowing corn or selling shoes—one cannot simply memorize a set of instructions; one has to practice the art himself. Ideally, such practice should involve apprenticing oneself to a master in the craft, watching him as he works and trying to imitate him. Consequently, when one wants to know what to do or how to proceed in a particular situation or set of circumstances, there is, in the final analysis, no other rule to follow save only this: Do what the expert would do.

So it is with the art of living. That is why Aristotle tends to reiterate what to many would seem rather obvious: in a moral or ethical situation, the thing to do is simply what the good man, or the man of sense and practical wisdom, would do. Or to express the same thing in terms of the doctrine of the mean: the mean between excess and defect in matters involving our desires and feelings and emotions is always what the good man would determine it to be.[2]

3. But ethics is not an art, at least not like other arts

However much considerations such as these may tend to reassure us that living wisely or well is after all but a matter of art and knowledge, there is no getting around the fact that morals or ethics, if it is an art, is not an art like the other arts. In fact, it is not solely, or even principally, an affair of skill or know-how at all. And so we are brought back once more to that somewhat enigmatic pronouncement of Aristotle's which we quoted earlier. Paraphrasing it rather freely, it states that, whereas in all the other arts a deliberate or voluntary mistake is much less serious than an involuntary one, in the art of living it is just the other way round. What does this mean?

4. Being a good man is different from being good at something: doing is more than knowing

Why is the practice of living to be judged by such different standards from those applicable to the building of bridges, the playing of basketball, the practice of medicine, or any other art? Why isn't it simply a case of a person's either knowing or not knowing how to live, just as it is a case of one's either knowing or not knowing how to play basketball, or how to perform an appendectomy, or how to build a bridge, or how to try a case? To live well, to be a good man, it would seem, one would need do no more than master the art of living, just as to be a good doctor, one need but master the art of medicine. Why not suppose that there is a simple and obvious parallel between the art of living and all the other arts? And yet the very homely considerations, at once so elementary and so undeniable, that we have just run through make us realize that this is impossible. But why?

The most obvious answer to this question is that, in the other arts, nothing is involved save knowledge and knowledge alone — i.e., knowledge in the sense of skill or know-how. But in living one's life, something else seems to be involved besides mere knowledge. As a first attempt at specifying what this "something else" is, one might put it that in order to live well or to be a good man, it is not enough merely to know how to live, to know what you need to do as a human being; in addition, you have to do it. In something like cabinet making, you may know how to ply your craft, but for one reason or another decide either not to do it, or else to do it badly. This would not in itself be any reflection upon your skill as a cabinet maker: you would still be competent; it's just that you had chosen not to display or exercise your competence. But in a moral or ethical context, a man who knew what he ought to do but chose not to do it would certainly not be a good man.

5. *Being a good man is different from being good at something: choosing is more than doing*

Perhaps, though, the contrast is not quite as simple as this. It's more than a simple difference between knowing and doing. For one thing, in the practical arts it is clear that there can never be a total or even a prolonged separation of knowing from doing. The knowledge that is involved in these arts is the sort that we call skill or know-how, and there just can't be any knowledge of this sort without doing. It is only through actually building bridges or practicing medicine or playing tennis that one becomes a bridge builder or a physician or a tennis player in the first place. And while one might cease for a time to use his skill without thereby immediately losing that skill, in the long run no one can continue to be a competent engineer or doctor or athlete without actually practicing his art.

For another thing, in the art of living, while in one sense it is correct to say that merely knowing what one ought to do without actually doing it does not suffice to make one a good man, in another sense whether one actually succeeds in doing what one intends to do or feels that one ought to do is at times quite irrelevant to being a good man or leading a good life. To take the most obvious sort of case: I may know that a friend of mine in San Francisco needs me badly and I may have every intention of going to his assistance, only to find that some outside factor such as a strike on the airlines, bad rail connections, or an automobile accident makes it impossible for me to arrive on time. In such a case, even though my knowing what I ought to do is not matched by my actually doing it, this would hardly constitute a reflection upon my character or my loyalty to my friend.

But if it is not a mere difference between knowing and doing that accounts for our differing standards of judgment in matters of skill, and in matters of morals, what does account for it? Does the difference lie in the fact that whereas in matters of skill it is know-how alone that counts, in matters of morals it is something more on the order of good intentions? But (for reasons that we shall consider later) such a way of formulating the difference between art and morals is somewhat over-simple and misleading. Instead, the difference is to be understood, not so much in terms of the distinction between knowing and choosing—more specifically, between knowing what needs to be done and actually wanting or choosing to do it.

A man is a good carpenter, we have said, if he knows how to do certain things. But whether he enjoys doing them, whether he chooses to do them well, whether he even chooses to do them at all—all this has nothing directly and immediately to do with his being skilled or competent in his art. On the other hand, for a man to be honest or fair or brave, it is not enough that he merely know what sort of behavior honesty and justice and bravery call for. In addition, he must actually choose to act this way himself. Not only that, but he must choose to do these things for their own sake. For a man who was honest enough in his dealings with others, not because he loved honesty, but only because he wanted to get ahead and be well thought of in the community, or because he was afraid that if he were dishonest, he might get caught—such a person we should hardly consider to be truly honest.

6. The Aristotelian distinction of moral virtues from intellectual virtues

Accordingly, taking cognizance of the peculiar requirements involved in being a good man as contrasted with those necessary for merely being a good craftsman, Aristotle insisted that to achieve the former one would need to cultivate not just certain habits of knowledge—the kind of knowledge called skill or know-how—but also certain habits of choice, the latter being known, in Aristotelian parlance, as moral virtues in contrast to the more familiar intellectual virtues, or habits of knowledge.

The word "virtue" itself may tend to stick in our craw in this day of disillusionment in general and of "angry young men" in particular. But in its original meaning the term does no more than point up the obvious fact that most of our human activities we can scarcely do at all, much less do them well, without first learning how. And such learned patterns of behavior, or acquired habits of action, as a result of which we come to be able to do well what otherwise we could not do at all, or at best could do only very badly—these are what Aristotle called "virtues."

7. The good man is no fool: no moral virtue without intellectual virtue

But the specific term "moral virtue" is likely to give rise to still further misunderstanding. For if we talk about habits of choice and learned patterns of behavior, which we call "moral virtue," we are apt to associate this with a picture of dear, good old Andy, who had "a heart full of gold," who never knowingly hurt a fly, but who was an impossible dullard and at times seemed hardly to have the sense to come in out of the rain!

But this is thoroughly to misconstrue the Aristotelian notion of moral virtue. The trouble seems to lie in the use of such expressions as "learned habits of choice" or "patterns of behavior." For such terms suggest to us choices and actions that are habitual in the sense of being mechanical and unthinking. But Aristotle had in mind something quite different. As he saw it, the reason the so-called moral virtues are needed for the good life is not that they will enable us to dispense with thinking and knowledge, but precisely and solely in order that such thought and knowledge may be brought to bear and become operative in our likes and dislikes and our choices of action. We shall then not merely know what the intelligent thing to do is, but we shall come to want it and actually choose to do it precisely because it is what intelligence dictates.

From this point of view, the honest man or the courageous man or the temperate person will not be one who has merely been conditioned to follow out unthinkingly certain approved patterns of behavior. He will be one who has learned how to let his choices and preferences be determined by such knowledge and understanding as he may have, rather than to proceed simply from chance feelings and impulses of the moment or from long established but mechanical habits of response.

For example, to revert to our earlier illustration, anyone will admit to having repeatedly had the distressing and often embarrassing experience of losing his temper and saying and doing things that were exceedingly foolish and unwise, which he himself soon came to regret. Accordingly the virtue of even temper may be understood as simply a learned response in which, instead of giving way to fits of temper, we allow our intelligence and better judgment to prevail. Nor is it otherwise with any of the other moral virtues. Courage, for instance, amounts to nothing more than a disposition to act rationally and intelligently in circumstances that appear to us frightening or alarming. Temperance is a disposition to respond in similar fashion in situations where we are subject to the physical attractions of food, drink, sex, etc. Likewise, as we have seen,[3] the virtue of self-respect, or *megalopsychia*, or whatever you choose to call it, is a virtue that disposes us to think neither too much nor too little of ourselves, but to be guided always by a just estimate of our own capacities and worth.

The moral virtues, then, are to be regarded simply as learned habits and dispositions that are directed solely toward letting reason and intelligence come into play in the determination of our choices of what to do and what not to do. From this point of view it could never properly be said of anyone that he was a man of excellent character, but at the same time a fool. For as Aristotle sees it, to be morally virtuous is precisely to be intelligent in one's behavior. Nor is there any other way for a man to be intelligent and wise in his conduct, save through the cultivation and exercise of the moral virtues. In short, to be brave, just, honest, temperate, even-tempered, modest, self-respecting is to be wise and intelligent in one's choices; and to be wise and intelligent in one's choices is to be brave, just, honest, temperate, and so on.

8. But isn't this right where we came in two chapters ago?

All this brings us back once again to some of the considerations raised in Chapter 2 regarding what it means to be human. For in Aristotle's account, we saw that being human or living a characteristically human existence, exercising the *ergon* or function that is appropriate to man—all this comes down to no more than living intelligently. A truly and properly human existence does not consist simply in being intelligent, in the sense of having a high I.Q. or having a lot of knowledge; rather it consists in living intelligently, in using one's intelligence in the conduct of one's life, in letting one's every choice be guided by such knowledge and understanding as one can bring to bear on the situation. But isn't this only another way of saying that being human consists in nothing more or less than the exercise of both intellectual and moral virtue—of intellectual virtue, because only so can a man be said to have knowledge and understanding; but also of moral virtue, because only so is one's knowledge brought to bear on his own life, suffusing and determining his conduct and even his choices and preferences?

9. Doubts and more doubts: can morals ever be supposed to rest ultimately upon knowledge?

With such a picture, however, contrast the following:

Badeau took Adams to the White House one evening and introduced him to President and Mrs. Grant. First and last, he saw a dozen Presidents at the White House, and the most famous were by no means the most agreeable, but he found Grant the most curious subject of study among them all. About no one did opinions differ so widely. Adams had no opinion, or occasion to make one. A single word with Grant satisfied him that, for his own good, the fewer words he risked the better. Thus far in life he had met with but one man of the same intellectual or unintellectual type—Garibaldi. Of the two, Garibaldi seemed to him a trifle the more intellectual, but, in both, the intellect counted for nothing; only the energy counted. The type was pre-intellectual, archaic, and would have seemed so even to the cave-dwellers. Adam, according to legend, was such a man.

In time one came to recognize the type in other men, with differences and variations, as normal; men whose energies were the greater, the less they wasted on thought; men who sprang from the soil to power; apt to be distrustful of themselves and of others; shy; jealous; sometimes vindictive; more or less dull in outward appearance; always needing stimulants, but for whom action was the highest stimulant—the instinct of fight. Such men were forces of nature, energies of the prime, like the *Pteraspis,* but they made short work of scholars. They had commanded thousands of such and saw no more in them than in others. The fact was certain; it crushed argument and intellect at once.[4]

Now making due allowance for Henry Adams' rather tortured and self-conscious predilection for contrasting the doer and the man of action with a Hamlet-like intellectual, the quoted passage does make it frighteningly clear how a man's life may be completely dominated and motivated by sheer unenlightened energy and drive—a life, indeed, in which such knowledge and intelligence and enlightenment as the man may have are all subordinated and put to the service of a more basic, but utterly blind and uncritical, impulse to act and to do.

Now in many ways this represents the very antithesis of the Socratic ideal of the examined life. Still, it is also a serious challenge. For one may ask, in the light of such an example, whether an examined or intelligent life in any such radical sense as Socrates would have it is really possible. Does it pertain to either the nature or the function of human intelligence to provide a guidance and direction to life that is ultimate and not merely relative and instrumental? Intelligence can tell us how to get what we want; but can it tell us what we really want or ought to want in the first place? Is not the posture of a Grant or a Garibaldi (supposing Adams' picture of them to have been a true one) much more in accordance with the realities of the human situation? If so, men's drives and impulses and inclinations must be taken as ultimate, and reason and intelligence must be regarded as merely instrumental in enabling us to attain whatever happens to appear valuable to us, not on the basis of any determinations of reason or intelligence, but merely on the basis of such affections and dispositions as may happen to characterize our particular natures.

Let us try to bring this issue to a head. The moral virtues, we have said, are nothing but habits of choice, such as will dispose us to choose those courses of action which intelligence and understanding prescribe. But do intelligence and reason ever really prescribe anything? Are they even capable of doing any more than describing what we are already inclined to do on other grounds?

For instance, take the virtue of courage. On the analysis we have given, to be brave is simply to be intelligent, i.e., in circumstances that seem dangerous or frightening the brave man is the one who chooses and acts in accordance with the dictates of intelligence. But think about this for a moment. Does it not grow increasingly dubious as one reflects upon it? For in what sense may intelligence be said to prescribe a courageous choice as being more intelligent and less stupid than a cowardly one? Certainly not in the sense in which a correct answer in arithmetic, say, is more intelligent than an incorrect one; or even in the sense in which one might say that a consideration of the evidence makes the hypothesis of a heliocentric universe a more intelligent one than of a geocentric universe.

Even the analogy with the arts seems to break down here. For although it certainly makes sense, in the context of an art such as surgery, to say that one way of performing an operation is more intelligent than another, this judgment is based on the presupposition that the operation is desirable in the first place. Moreover, in all the arts, it would seem that any judgment as to what is the more or less intelligent way of doing something is based on a prior assumption of some desired end or goal. Must it not then be concluded that intelligence can prescribe what is better or worse on the presupposition of a prior inclination or desire which determines the end, and which intelligence subserves only as an instrument for calculating the means? But if so, then the Socratic project of an examined life would appear to be, in the last analysis, utterly futile: the end we seek is determined by irrational, or at least pre-rational, motives, and intelligence can only prescribe the best means to such ends.

10. In defense of rationality: man's end or goal is a rationally defensible one

But this sort of criticism obviously rests upon a misunderstanding. True, human reason and human intelligence do not determine human values in the sense of creating them; rather their job is simply to discover such values. Moreover, when reason sets about to discover what the good life for man is, or what the characteristically human good is, then the results of the investigation, we would suggest, will be along such lines as we indicated in our second chapter. The human good will be found to be that natural end toward which a human being is oriented by virtue of being human, as an acorn is oriented toward its natural end by virtue of its nature as an acorn. In this sense, man's end, the goal or purpose of human life, is something given; it is a fact of nature. Reason or intelligence may be said to determine what this natural end is only in the sense of discovering or recognizing it, not in the sense of creating or positing it.

Suppose we push this consideration to the point of a seeming paradox. We could say that this natural end or natural disposition of a human being is something pre-rational and pre-intelligent: it is just a fact which reason can do no more than recognize. And yet—and here is the decisive point—having come to recognize this pre-rational and pre-intelligent end, our human intelligence then sees that it is man's natural end and hence the proper end for a human being to seek. It thus becomes an end which we do not seek merely in fact and automatically, toward which we are impelled uncritically and unreflectingly, but rather an end which we see that we have reason to seek and which we recognize as being the right and proper end for us as human beings. In this latter sense, then, such an end is seen to be a rational end, i.e., an end which can be justified and defended as being worthy of our seeking or as being right for us to seek. It is in these terms that the attitude and performance of a Socrates are to be distinguished from and vindicated against those of a Grant or a Garibaldi.

11. In defense of rationality: the rationally defensible end or goal of man is to be rational

As we saw in our earlier investigation, when we turn to the question of what this natural, and hence rationally justifiable, end for man consists in, we find that it consists precisely in not settling for any end save one that is rationally justifiable—that is, it consists in living intelligently and leading an examined life. Man's natural end, on this view, turns out to be that of being the sort of person who is not content merely to go on doing or seeking that which he is naturally impelled to do or to seek, or which he has always been in the habit of doing or seeking, but without knowing why. Rather the good man is the man who knows and understands why he does what he does, and who, instead of acting blindly, has a reason for doing what he does.

Unhappily, though, in thus attempting to characterize man's proper end and goal as being both naturally determined and intelligently determined at one and the same time, it is difficult to obviate the kind of misunderstanding that springs from a certain ambiguity in the words "natural" and "nature" when used in this connection. On the one hand, we say that the right and honorable thing to do is that which one tends to do or is impelled to do simply by nature. On the other hand, we are equally insistent that in so far as it is human nature that is involved, to do that which one tends to do naturally but without recognizing that it is thus natural and without understanding that it is therefore the right and reasonable thing to do—this is not to behave intelligently, and hence, for a human being, is not even to behave in a way that is natural. In short, for a human being the end can be an intelligent one only in so far as it is rationally recognized and intelligently appreciated as being in this way the natural end for man.

Further, when a man thus becomes intelligently aware of what the natural goal for him as a human being is, he sees that, so far as its content is concerned, what this natural human end consists in is simply to live intelligently. There is thus a two-fold sense in which, on Aristotle's view, the natural goal or end of man is a rational and intelligent one. It is intelligent in that it is rationally defensible and justifiable: we can see why it is the true and proper end for us, simply because it is the natural end for us. And also, it is intelligent in that what this end consists in and what it calls upon a man to be and to do is simply to be intelligent and to live intelligently. That is to say, the rationally defensible and justifiable end for a human being is simply to be as rational and intelligent as possible in all that he chooses and does.

12. How that which is morally wrong can be said to be a mistake or an error

Assuming, then, that our end or goal consists simply in being intelligent, let us try to arrive at a better understanding of that seeming paradox, according to which being virtuous amounts to no more than being intelligent and being intelligent amounts simply to being virtuous.

What must bother anyone about such a formula is the question of whether and how the virtuous course of action can be regarded as simply the action which intelligence dictates. However much we may admire and respect qualities such as bravery, loyalty, personal integrity, and reliability, why should it be supposed that to exhibit such qualities is the same thing as being intelligent?

Let us remind ourselves of our earlier examples of men whose conduct and general behavior were such as to be adjudged foolish and unwise. It strikes us as being natural and proper to say that Sir Walter Elliott was an ass, that Charles I was curiously deluded and erected his whole life upon a mistake, or that C. P. Snow's Mr. Nightingale was unwise in his conduct of life, in fact, that his whole outlook was twisted and mistaken. In cases like these we apply to the characters and behavior of human beings epithets like "mistaken," "in error," "dead wrong," etc., which are borrowed from the purely intellectual realm. Yet the mistakes that are involved in such men's lives do not seem altogether comparable to mistakes in arithmetic, say, or in the sciences or technical arts.

Very well, then, let us look more closely at just what it means to be wrong or mistaken in one's behavior and in one's character. In saying that Sir Walter or King Charles or Nightingale made mistakes or got on the wrong track, do we not mean that they were woefully ignorant of the truth about themselves, that they did not know what was best for them? "If only they could see themselves as others see them," one is tempted to say.

13. What is it to know or not to know the truth about oneself?

What is this truth about themselves of which we say they were ignorant, and what is it that is best for them and that they don't seem to know about? To answer the latter question in a thoroughly Socratic manner, what is best for any human being is that he live intelligently, that he lead an examined life. But this means that instead of acting blindly from impulse or uncritically from mere force of habit, a man should act from knowledge and understanding.

Presumably, therefore, from Socrates' standpoint, the fact that our three characters did not know what was best for them could mean only that they did not realize the importance of having intelligent reasons for ordering their lives—that, instead, their general behavior was fundamentally blind and unthinking, proceeding largely from their feelings of vanity, pride, timidity, resentment.

Why is behavior that proceeds from mere impulse, passion, or force of habit to be considered blind or ignorant? The Socratic answer must be that it is behavior which the individual has not bothered to think through or to justify or to give reasons for. This is not to say that there are never good reasons for one's doing what one is simply impelled to do or has merely been in the habit of doing. The point is that so long as one does not know what these reasons are, and goes ahead and acts not knowing what they are, then to this extent one is not acting like an intelligent and rational man.

Of course, more often than not, when we act merely from impulse or from habit, what we do is not only something for which we give no reason, but also something for which we *could* give no reason, or only a rationalization. But what would a good reason be? How is one to justify one's choices so as to bring them up to this standard of a truly intelligent, thinking human being in the Socratic sense? The answer that we are about to give may seem more like begging the question than answering it. Yet in the final analysis, any justification of one's actions, at least if it proceeds on Socratic lines, must come down to this: this choice or that act is justified if it is one that is consonant with or contributes to an examined life, i.e., if it proceeds from no other motive save that of wanting to be a truly human being, of wanting to act rationally and intelligently and in the light of such knowledge and understanding as one can muster.

"But," you will say, "on such a basis almost anyone can justify almost anything he does. Few men consider themselves to be unintelligent and unthinking. Indeed, Sir Walter Elliott no doubt thought himself an eminently reasonable and intelligent man. He would have been the first to claim that reason and understanding, not prejudice and passion, were his sole guides to action."

The answer to this is that Sir Walter may have thought himself intelligent, but in fact he was not. He may have thought that his only motive in life was to be a man of reason and understanding, but it is all too patent that his real motive was simply vanity. Indeed, this is how Jane Austen was able to make Sir Walter appear such a fool: he was utterly fooled about himself; in the sense of the Socratic injunction, he was not a man who had ever bothered to know himself at all.

14. Moral error and intellectual error — the same and yet not the same

But don't we have right here the answer to the question that has been vexing us for so long? Sir Walter did not know the truth about himself, and because of this ignorance his character, far from being admirable, was absurd and ridiculous. Yet his error was certainly no mere intellectual one. One might say that his whole life was one long mistake, but it was not the same kind of mistake as an error in long division or in foretelling a decline in the stock market.

What sort of mistake was it, then? This concerns not only Sir Walter's error, but King Charles' or Nightingale's or Grant's or yours or mine. May we not say that a mistake of this sort consists not so much in not being able intellectually to see or know the truth about oneself, as in not being willing or disposed to see this truth? To put it a little differently, a man falls into error of this sort not from intellectual weakness, but from having allowed his feelings and passions, rather than his knowledge and understanding, to determine his choices. In other words, this kind of error involves what Aristotle called moral virtue, as much as intellectual virtue.

The same point is borne out when we consider how the ignorance and error that make for folly in human character are to be removed. Again, this is no mere affair of an intellectual passage from ignorance to knowledge. Nor is the purpose of such a removal simply the acquisition of information and knowledge. The fool who is brought to see the truth about himself is not like the young physics student who is brought to see the truth of the quantum theory. The reason for this difference is that, as Aristotle remarks, in a science such as ethics the end is not knowledge but action.[5]

So when we ask: do morals and ethics rest upon knowledge, is the good life an affair of knowing and knowing how? The answer clearly is "Yes." But the "knowing" that is here needed is a knowing that is inseparable from choosing, just as the choosing must be one that is based on knowing. Of the two, the choosing is the far more difficult to bring off. To make the point in Aristotle's own words:

> Nor will the suggested analogy with the arts bear scrutiny. A work of art is good or bad in itself—let it possess a certain quality, and that is all we ask of it. But virtuous actions are not done in a virtuous— a just or temperate—way merely because they have the appropriate quality. The doer must be in a certain frame of mind when he does them. Three conditions are involved. (1) The agent must act in full consciousness of what he is doing. (2) He must "will" his action, and will it for its own sake. (3) The act must proceed from a fixed and unchangeable disposition. Now these requirements, if we except mere knowledge, are not counted among the necessary qualifications of an artist. For the acquisition of virtue, on the other hand, knowledge is of little or no value, but the other requirements are of immense, of sovran, importance, since it is the repeated performance of just and temperate actions that produces virtue. Actions, to be sure, are called just and temperate when they are such as a just or temperate man would do. But the doer is just or temperate not because he does such things but when he does them in the way of just and temperate persons.[6]

5

Failure and Unhappiness: Are They Our Own Responsibility?

1. Human failure, its nature and causes

In earlier chapters there has been much talk of human folly. To the more cynical this might seem to be only laboring the obvious. But to the more philosophical, it raises some interesting questions. Is it true that anybody who isn't happy is a fool? In many ways this could perhaps be said to epitomize Aristotelian moral theory. On such a view, moral principles and moral rules, if they are legitimate and defensible ones, are not just so many edicts imposed upon the individual from the outside, whether it be by parents or by society or by God Himself. Rather, moral rules are more in the nature of counsels of perfection or instructions as to what one ought or ought not to do in order to attain happiness.

But if learning how to live be no more than what is in one's own best interests, and if not learning be not so much "morally wrong," in the currently popular sense of that term, as simply foolish, then how does it happen that so many of us fail to learn? For most of us do fail; we don't lead examined lives; we don't achieve our natural human perfection; we can't honestly say that we are happy, at least not in any distinctively human way. What are the reasons and sources of such failure? Is it a failure that we could have prevented or that we might still do something about? Is it the sort of thing for which we may hold only ourselves responsible?

If we confine ourselves to generalities, it is not hard to classify the main causes of our failure to behave wisely, to make the most of ourselves, to attain true human happiness. In the light of what we have said thus far about man's nature and the human situation, these causes fall readily under three main headings. A man's failure to attain his end may be due either to ignorance (he doesn't know what the true end or goal is of human existence, or else he doesn't know how to attain it); or to bad choices (he knows what the end is and what it takes to achieve it, but he just doesn't choose to do it); or to bad luck and the sheer force of circumstances (he knows what to do, and wants to do it, but he is prevented by purely external forces from carrying out his intention).

Accordingly, on the score of responsibility, the question becomes whether it is our own fault that we fail, when such failure is due either to not knowing what we ought to do, or to not choosing to do it, or to being prevented from doing it.

2. *Is ignorance an excuse?*

Suppose we consider first the sort of failure that is due to ignorance. Can we really be blamed if we make fools of ourselves and throw away our lives, simply because we don't know any better? How many people really know, or have ever even stopped to think, what is really best for them? Ask the next person you meet on the street whether or not he is aware that only the examined life is worth living. He will think you are crazy. What do the claims of Socratic self-knowledge mean to him? He has never even heard of Socrates, much less taken his message to heart.

Nevertheless, the matter may not be quite so simple after all. In order to open up some of the complexities that are involved in failures arising from ignorance, suppose we consider how the issue tends to present itself in legal contexts, which are somewhat analogous to moral or ethical contexts. Thus in Western society the traditions of both civil law and common law have always tended to recognize the validity of the two maxims:

1. *Ignorantia legis neminem excusat.*
2. *Ignorantia facti excusat.*

Ignorance of the law does not excuse, but ignorance of fact does. What does this distinction mean, and why should only the latter be considered excusable and not the former?

A. IGNORANCE OF FACT

The stock example of ignorance of fact is a man out hunting: he hears a movement in the thicket, he fires; but instead of shooting a deer, he shoots a fellow hunter. Is the first hunter to be held responsible for the injury inflicted on the second? The first man can say that he did not intend to injure anyone; he was only shooting at what he thought was a deer. Was it, then, just an accident, regrettable of course, but not anything for which anyone could be blamed or held accountable?

So far as the legal situation goes, the answer to such a question would doubtless turn on whether or not the man who had done the shooting had acted recklessly or carelessly. Had he, even though he knew the danger involved, fired just as soon as he saw the slightest movement in the bushes, without bothering to take precautions? Or had he, because of his excitement and eagerness, fired precipitately and without stopping to think whether there was any possible danger involved? On the former alternative, the man would be held to have acted recklessly, since he was aware of the risks he was taking in such hasty firing. On the latter alternative, he would be held to have been careless or negligent, since he did not stop to think either of risks or of precautions.

A third alternative is possible: that the hunter not only was aware of the dangers involved, but took the necessary precautions; that he did not fire until he actually saw the antlers of the deer; but at that very instant, quite by accident, the second hunter moved into his line of fire. Under such circumstances the first man would hardly be held accountable for the injury done to the second.

When the transition is made from a legal to an ethical context, our assessments would not be very different. Recklessness and carelessness could well be considered as moral weaknesses, or, more accurately, as evidences of either a lack of, or else of a failure to exercise, certain moral virtues.

It is also conceivable that even in a moral context there would be situations in which injury or harm might come to a man *because* he was exercising the moral virtues. Suppose a driver going north on the New Jersey Turnpike begins to run into patches of fog as he moves into the marshy flats on the approaches to New York City. Obedient to the specially posted traffic warnings, he reduces his speed, takes the requisite precautions, and alerts himself to possible dangers. Suddenly a heavy truck, coming up from behind and going at top speed, but quite invisible because of a sudden patch of dense fog, crashes into the rear of the car. One might say that had the driver of the car not been proceeding in a calm, cautious, intelligent manner, had he been either more reckless or more careless than he was, the truck would never have caught up with him, and the accident would never have occurred. The driver of the car would certainly not be held legally responsible for the accident; nor could he be held morally responsible for anything that by any stretch of the imagination could be considered foolish or improper behavior—but this would doubtless seem small consolation for having one's car demolished and being obliged to spend several months in the hospital recovering from serious injuries. The wages of sin may be death, but so may the wages of virtue.

Leaving it to the cynics to do what they will with such a hypothetical case, the fact remains that in morals and ethics, the principle that governs the assessment of responsibility for ignorance of fact is a very simple one. Clearly, we are responsible, we are to blame, if our ignorance is due to a lack of moral virtue—for example, when we don't know the facts of the situation because we were too lazy to find out, or deliberately avoided finding out for fear the knowledge might be disagreeable, or were simply reckless or careless, or because we placed a wrong construction upon the facts, or because we were stampeded, so to speak, by our emotions: fear, anger, lust, jealousy, resentment, or whatnot. It is a truism that our judgment of things is often colored, or distorted, or blinded by how we feel, by our passions and appetites. Accordingly, when we fail to appreciate correctly, or maybe even to appreciate at all, the facts in a given situation, simply because we have not learned to moderate and redirect our feelings and desires so as to bring them under the control of intelligence and understanding, then surely we are responsible for such ignorance.

On the other hand, there is no getting around the fact that human life being what it is, there will be countless situations in our lives where, as we say, we would never have acted as we did, had we known what the facts were, and yet where at the same time we couldn't possibly have been expected to know what the facts were, however constant and efficient we might have been in the exercise of moral virtue. Unforeseeable and, in a moral sense at least, unavoidable harms and injuries do befall us; nor in such cases are we properly to blame for the consequences of our ignorance.

B. IGNORANCE OF LAW

But what now of ignorance of law? This is in many ways a more difficult principle to deal with, as is indicated by the fact that its explanation and justification are a source of no little embarrassment to the lawyers themselves. "Ignorance of the law," they say, "is never an excuse." But why? Unfortunately, legal scholars do not seem too ready to come forward with a justification of the maxim, unless it be in terms of social utility: society, it is argued, cannot be maintained unless there is some system of legal order; and a system of legal order cannot be maintained unless every individual citizen is held responsible for a knowledge of the law. But while this may be all very well from the standpoint of society, it seems rather harsh from the standpoint of justice to the individual. When we consider the volumes upon volumes of existing statutes, court decisions interpreting the statutes, and the equally voluminous works expounding the tradition of the common law, it would appear to be not merely a fiction but a downright injustice to presume that every man shall know the law. Moreover, what the law is in a given area is likely to be upset any day by a new court decision, and that decision in turn may be upset by an appeal to a still higher court, the parties to the litigation, notwithstanding, being presumed to have known all the while what the law was, even in advance of such judicial pronouncements and reversals—all this would appear to compound both the fiction and the injustice to the point of making them intolerable.

When we come to morals and ethics, there tends to arise a somewhat comparable embarrassment in connection with the ethical analogue of *Ignorantia legis neminem excusat.* For in the moral realm, there does seem to be operative a sort of natural law, in contrast to the more positive law that prevails in the legal order. Indeed, the very same principles of morals and ethics that we have thus far been concerned to defend could all be regarded as so many natural laws, or laws determined by man's nature. For instance, we have argued that it pertains to the very nature of man that a full life for a human being must consist in living intelligently. Likewise, it is a law of man's nature that he cannot lead an examined or intelligent life without first learning how to do so. And it is a further law of human nature that in order to be a good man, as distinct from merely being a good artisan, something more has to be acquired besides mere know-how, habits of choice or moral virtues being equally necessary.

To be sure, the language of "natural law" has gone out of fashion nowadays. Hence it may strike us as a bit awkward, not to say unnatural, to use a seemingly legal language in connection with the living of one's life and with the demands and requirements of one's human nature. But such a feeling of strangeness may be no more than a prejudice due to accidents of fashion. At any rate, for our present purposes it should prove illuminating to employ such legal-sounding language in connection with ethics. Thus we can say that the moral obligations and requirements of human life are determined by nothing less than the laws of man's nature and of the order of nature generally.

Very well, then, what about a man's responsibility for ignorance of such natural moral laws? Can it be maintained that every human being is presumed to know what such laws are and that ignorance of them is something for which there is no excuse?

At first glance it might seem that posing such questions would only serve to raise the ghost of relativism all over again. Given the bewildering variety of conditions, customs, mores, ideals, and circumstances of life that have characterized man in the course of his history, how can one possibly claim that only one way of life, the so-called intelligent or examined life, is natural to man? But a little closer examination will soon disclose that the question raised here is not one of relativism; it is this: Supposing that there is a natural law which determines what the right life for man is, how can all men be expected to know what it is? A primitive South Sea islander, a completely brainwashed North Korean Communist, an ignorant serf brought up in the confining conditions of a medieval manor, a young Puerto Rican immigrant living in grinding poverty in a Harlem slum, a slave laborer in ancient Egypt, a picked member of the Hitler Jugend, whose whole life has been one continuous process of being conditioned to a blind acceptance of the Nazi ideal—how could it possibly be maintained that human beings such as these, straitened and confined as they are, are in a position to know and appreciate the Socratic ideal of the examined life? Put this way, the thing certainly does seem preposterous. Nor is there any doubt that responsibility for ignorance on the part of those in less favorable circumstances of life is less than those in more favorable circumstances. It must doubtless be admitted that there are cases where the conditions of human life are such that anything like responsibility for ignorance of the so-called natural laws of human existence cannot fairly be attributed to the individuals in question.

At the same time, it is easy to exaggerate the prevalence of conditions of life so extreme as to remove altogether a man's responsibility for knowing what the score is in human existence, or what are the natural obligations that are incumbent upon a human being for the perfection of his own nature. For take the case even of a slave, ignorant and uneducated and living in conditions of the utmost degradation. Would anyone make bold to say that such a man was totally incapable of recognizing instances of human vanity and folly, of cowardice and courage, of meanness and generosity?

It is true that as the conditions of life vary from age to age, from region to region, or from one culture to another, the criteria of bravery, say, or of honesty, or of stupidity, will vary considerably. But the distinction between bravery and cowardice, honesty and dishonesty, wisdom and folly, will nonetheless be recognized and maintained almost universally.

In fact, it stands to reason that when the standard of perfection in human life is simply to live wisely or intelligently, the intelligent course of action in one set of circumstances will be very different from what it is in another. The intelligent life for a Tibetan monk will take a somewhat different form from that appropriate to an American businessman. But even though our recognition of wisdom or folly in others may falter at times or even fail completely, particularly if the circumstances of their exhibition are radically different from those that we ourselves are accustomed to, still is it not possible for us usually to win through to at least some sort of appreciation of human excellence, or of human stupidity, no matter how superficially different our own standards may be?

Suppose we try an experiment in support of this contention. Suppose we consider the characters of certain historical figures, widely separated from one another in time, in geography, in culture and civilization, and in the specific circumstances of their lives. And as we consider such examples, suppose we keep putting to ourselves the question whether, just as we ourselves, despite our distance and difference from the men we are considering, are able to appreciate the excellence or the deficiency of their characters—whether these same men themselves, had they been able to know about one another, would not have likewise responded to one another's excellences or deficiencies.

As our first example, let us again consider the character of Socrates, this time as he himself recounts it when speaking in his own defense at his trial:

> Let me relate to you a passage of my own life which will prove to you that I should never have yielded to injustice from any fear of death, and that "as I should have refused to yield" I must have died at once. I will tell you a tale of the courts, not very interesting perhaps, but nevertheless true. The only office of state which I ever held, O men of Athens, was that of senator: the tribe Antiochis, which is my tribe, had the presidency at the trial of the generals who had not taken up the bodies of the slain after the battle of Arginusae; and you proposed to try them in a body, contrary to law, as you all thought afterwards; but at the time I was the only one of the Prytanes who was opposed to the illegality, and I gave my vote against you; and when the orators threatened to impeach and arrest me, and you called and shouted, I made up my mind that I would run the risk, having law and justice with me, rather than take part in your injustice because I feared imprisonment and death. This happened in the days of the democracy. But when the oligarchy of the

Thirty was in power, they sent for me and four others into the ro-tunda, and bade us bring Leon the Salaminian from Salamis, as they wanted to put him to death. This was a specimen of the sort of com-mands which they were always giving with the view of implicating as many as possible in their crimes; and then I showed, not in word only but in deed, that, if I may be allowed to use such an expres-sion, I cared not a straw for death, and that my great and only care was lest I should do an unrighteous or unholy thing. For the strong arm of that oppressive power did not frighten me into doing wrong; and when we came out of the rotunda the other four went to Sala-mis and fetched Leon, but I went quietly home. For which I might have lost my life, had not the power of the Thirty shortly afterwards come to an end. And many will witness to my words.[1]

For our second example we shall shift the scene from Athens in 399 B.C. to the civil wars in Great Britain in the seventeenth century. The following is a brief account by a modern historian of the character of a certain James Butler, Earl of Ormonde, whom the King had placed in command of his forces in Ireland. Perhaps it should be noted in passing that at this time the fighting in Ireland had amounted to a veri-table "fury of destruction and hatred," Irish against English, Catholic against Protestant, and Parliament sympathizers against the forces of the King. This, then, is the sketch given of Ormonde:

> The Earl of Ormonde, general of the forces of the Dublin Gov-ernment, refused to lay waste Irish villages or kill civilians. The greater number of his Norman-Irish family were in sympathy with the rebels; his mother was a Roman Catholic, his brother was in arms with the insurgents. He had other anxieties, for the King had certainly communicated secrets to him that he would have been happier not to have known and he, if anyone, knew the extent of Charles's inept tampering with the Irish. His competence and popu-larity with the Government forces made him indispensable, yet there were those on the Council who suspected him of complicity with the rebels. But Ormonde stood with great steadfastness, for law, order and loyalty to the Crown, and rebutted the whispered slanders: "I will go on constantly," he wrote, "neither sparing the

rebel because he is my kinsman, or was my friend, nor yet will I one jot the more sharpen my sword to satisfy anybody but myself in the faithful performance of my charge."

His wife was cut off in Kilkenny Castle with her children and the hundreds of fugitives whom she had received and relieved there. The Irish leaders threatened to destroy them unless Ormonde abandoned his command of the Government forces. The English responded that if the Countess and her children came to harm, no Irish woman or child would be spared. But Ormonde, not slackening his preparations for the spring campaign, proclaimed a different answer. If his wife and children, he wrote, "shall receive injury by men, I shall never revenge it on women and children; which, as it would be base and un-Christian, would be extremely below the price I value my wife and children at."[2]

Placing the characters of these two men, Socrates and the Earl of Ormonde, side by side, it goes almost without saying that there is a vast difference between fifth-century Athens after the death of Pericles and seventeenth-century Britain and Ireland under Charles I. Likewise it goes without saying that it would be hard to imagine men more different in many ways than Socrates and Ormonde—the one a *pöbelhafter Mensch* as Nietzsche called him, the son of a midwife, whose speech was ever that used "in the agora, at the tables of the money changers";[3] the other a refined and elegant Anglo-Irish aristocrat, nurtured in baroque surroundings and moving in a society where civility and good manners must have been absolutely *de rigueur*. Yet despite their differences—or perhaps one should say *in* their very differences—both men are at one in their determination to maintain their sanity and judgment in the face of pressures, passions, betrayals, and even the fear of death itself. It is just this sort of thing that the intelligent life and the virtuous life consist in.

Moreover, in the context of our present argument, what is significant is not merely the fact that both Socrates and Ormonde, each in their respective ways, might be said to have lived examined lives, but also that we today as we read the accounts of such lives are able to appreciate the excellence of their examples. For in the circumstances and conditions of our lives we are as different from both Socrates and

Ormonde as they were from each other. Yet the requirements of human excellence are discernible in human life wherever it may be found, with the result that we all, with but few exceptions, have at least some inkling of the kinds of claims which our very human nature makes upon us.

Otherwise, how should we ever be able to read history and literature, not merely with aesthetic appreciation, but with an appreciation of their relevance to our own lives? The fact of our human response to examples of human achievement or human failure, of human wisdom or human folly, no matter how different these others may be from us in time or place or culture or circumstances of life—this fact is of no little import, when it comes to deciding whether there are more or less objective standards of human excellence and whether, as men, we are capable of recognizing such standards.

To be sure, many of us may have become so benumbed by the ordinary business and drudgery, to say nothing of the ordinary pleasures and distractions, of life that we have ceased to respond to, or perhaps even to be aware of, the claims that our own human nature makes upon us. Even so, most of us tend to be uncomfortably, even if dimly, conscious of how we could have fostered and cultivated such an awareness, instead of disregarding or even blinding ourselves to what, simply as human beings, we might have been, and should have been, and perhaps could still become, if we chose.

Lest it be thought that in our experiment we have limited ourselves to such characters as could evoke only our respect and approval, we might end with the following estimate which Dr. Johnson once gave of the character of Falstaff.

> But Falstaff, unimitated, unimitable Falstaff, how shall I describe thee! thou compound of sense and vice; of sense which may be admired, but not esteemed; of vice which may be despised, but hardly detested. Falstaff is a character loaded with faults, and with those faults which naturally produce contempt. . . . Yet the man thus corrupt, thus despicable, makes himself necessary to the prince that despises him, by the most pleasing of all qualities, perpetual gaiety, by an unfailing power of exciting laughter, which is the more freely indulged, as his wit is not of the splendid or ambitious kind, but con-

sists in easy scapes and sallies of levity, which make sport, but raise no envy. It must be observed, that he is stained with no enormous or sanguinary crimes, so that his licentiousness is not so offensive but that it may be borne for his mirth.

The moral to be drawn from this representation is, that no man is more dangerous than he that, with a will to corrupt, hath the power to please; and that neither wit nor honesty ought to think themselves safe with such a companion, when they see Henry seduced by Falstaff.[4]

May we not conclude that despite diversity of periods and cultures, despite the seeming heterogeneity of moral standards and standards of value, human beings do nevertheless seem capable—not infallibly, and certainly not unanimously, but still with impressive regularity—of appreciating and responding to instances of human worth and human weakness, of human perfection and human imperfection, wherever found? It is this universal, if intermittent, power of mutual appreciation among men which renders us capable of such pursuits as history and the humanities, and without which, though we might become scientists, we could never become humanists, or perhaps even human beings in the true sense.

Moreover—and with this we return to the central argument of the present section—if all men do have such a power of mutual appreciation, an ability to recognize and respond to both human folly and human excellence, then it would seem that what we have termed "ignorance of law," in the sense of an ignorance of the laws and values of our own human nature, is an ignorance for which all of us are in a measure responsible, and for which we are to be held more or less accountable, however much that responsibility and accountability may vary in degree, depending on the particular circumstances of our various human conditions.

3. Which is prior, ignorance as the cause of moral failure, or moral weakness as the cause of ignorance?

What has been established in the preceding section is that, given the normal human condition, nearly all of us probably do know, at least in principle, what is best for us. We are also capable of knowing, at least much of the time, what is the better course to follow even in a concrete particular case. Hence if many of us fail to become good men largely because of ignorance of what we ought to do, it must be that such ignorance, far from being an ultimate principle of explanation, is self-caused and self-imposed—i.e., an ignorance that we have brought upon ourselves and for which we ourselves are responsible. To put the same point a little differently, in the final analysis our human failures are ultimately due not to the fact that we don't know what we ought to do, but rather to the fact that we don't choose to act on our knowledge.

We are, then, brought face to face with that second cause of failure, mentioned earlier, which now bids fair to absorb, even to displace, ignorance as a cause of failure in anything like an ultimate sense. What we said earlier was that our bad choices, quite as much as our ignorance, might be the source of our failures. But it appears that even when ignorance is the cause of failure, it is usually an ignorance which is due to our bad choices. Accordingly, it begins to look as if right choice, much more than right knowledge, were the primary concern of ethics and morals.

4. Plato's puzzler: virtue is nothing but knowledge, and vice nothing but ignorance

But no sooner do we make this suggestion than we are sure to find ourselves embarrassed by any such notion of human choice, for its understanding is fraught with any number of difficulties and complications. There seems to be no better way of broaching some of these complications than to consider briefly the famous thesis, defined in Plato's dialogue of the *Protagoras*, that virtue is knowledge.[5] The upshot of this Platonic thesis is that everything we have just been saying about choice, rather than ignorance, being the ultimate cause of failure is so much stuff and nonsense! Instead, Plato's view in the *Protagoras* seems to be that failure can have no other cause than ignorance, and that the only reason anybody ever makes a bad choice is simply because he does not know any better.

More specifically, Plato takes his stand on the proposition that it is impossible for anyone ever knowingly to make a bad or wrong choice. For what is it to make such a choice, if not to choose that which turns out to be bad or injurious or harmful to the chooser? And who would ever deliberately choose that which he knew would be detrimental to himself? It is true that we often deliberately submit to that which we know will be hurtful and disagreeable. But is not this always with a view to what we think will in the long run be of greater benefit—as, for instance, when we undergo the suffering of a surgical operation, but only for the sake of regaining our health? Or if we don't actually believe that the course of action we are choosing will in the long run be of greater benefit to us, we at least are convinced that in the short run it will have some advantage, and that in the long run it probably won't hurt or make too much difference. Hence we say to ourselves, "Why not try to get such short-run enjoyment and benefit as we can? Surely, it will be worth it." Such is the way we usually reason. Is it even conceivable that a man would ever choose that which he was quite certain would be more harmful to him than not, without any compensating factor to make the venture seem worth while after all?

Or look at it this way. What precisely does it mean for us to choose one thing or one course of action over another? Does it not mean that we prefer the one to the other? But to prefer one thing to another means that we take the one to be somehow better than the other. And when it is said that we "take" one thing to be better or preferable, this means that it *seems* better to us, we *think* it better. Indeed, is it any more than a tautology to say of human choice that it is always a choosing of that which seems or appears better to us? Of course, it may not really be better, but only seem so. And yet this but tends to confirm Plato's thesis. For Plato is not for a minute contending that no one ever does in fact choose what is worse rather than what is better; his contention is only that no one ever does so knowingly. Consequently, for him, all of the bad choices which we human beings make—and goodness knows we make enough of them!—turn out to be but a function of our not knowing any better.

But doesn't this conclusion run directly counter to what our experience repeatedly attests? Have we not all upon occasion said to ourselves: "I see what the better course is and I approve it, but I follow the worse" (*"Video meliora proboque deteriora sequor"*)?

Nor is it merely to common sense that this Platonic thesis does violence. In addition, it runs counter to Aristotle's contention, which we explained and defended so painstakingly in the preceding chapter, that for the leading of a good or happy life, it will not suffice to have only intellectual virtue; one must have moral virtue as well. But now Plato comes along and says that whatever the better course of action may be, if a man knows what this is, he will necessarily follow it; on the other hand, if a man does something that is bad or foolish, this can only be because he didn't realize what he was doing. What else, in fact, could be the sense of the celebrated Platonic maxim that virtue is simply a matter of knowledge and vice of ignorance? Similarly, on this Platonic view, the business of living well turns out to be a mere matter of skill or know-how, and of nothing else—just like the other arts.

5. Is there no getting around Plato's argument?

How is one to meet this Platonic thesis? For however many grounds we may have for thinking it dubious, or even sophistic, it is extremely difficult to refute. Suppose we try to counter Plato's thesis by appealing to the consideration that ignorance, so far from being the only reason for our bad choices, is itself not infrequently the result of our own choices. After all, human knowledge, and correspondingly human ignorance, do not arise in a complete vacuum. Much, if not most, of our knowledge results from our having deliberately chosen to inform ourselves and to find out about things. And as for ignorance, we have already remarked on how often it is that we don't know about something, for the reason that we did not choose to take the trouble to learn, or perhaps because we deliberately chose not to learn. Indeed, the more one considers the matter, the more it seems that our ignorances and stupidities are perhaps mainly due to our own laziness, or maybe fear, or smugness, or carelessness. Hence why not turn the tables on Plato and say that it is not because of ignorance that our characters are weak and our choices bad, but rather because our characters are weak that we are so much of the time ignorant of what we should know and could know?

But Plato could have an easy answer for this one—although by now our interpretation of Plato has far outrun the actual Platonic texts. Plato need only point out that it merely shifts the issue of the decisive role of knowledge and ignorance in moral behavior to a further remove, but does not eliminate it. Granted that my lack of knowledge may be due to my not choosing to find out, or perhaps to my not choosing to consider what I very well know, still what about this prior matter of my not choosing to find out, or of my not choosing to exercise the knowledge I have? Why did I not choose to do so? Surely if I had realized (i.e., if I had known) how important it was to find out, or how much better it would have been for me to bring to bear the knowledge I already had, then most assuredly I would have chosen to do so. But I did not realize and didn't know; hence I didn't choose. Once again, the principle becomes both plain and inescapable: any choice necessarily presupposes some sort of judgment as to better and worse; and whether the judgment be a true or a false one is a matter of whether one knows or doesn't know. In other words, virtue or right choice is simply a matter of knowing what the right thing to do is, just as not making the right choice is simply a matter of not knowing.

There doesn't seem to be any way of penetrating Plato's defenses. For no sooner does one adduce evidence to show that some such factor as bad choice enters into our human failures, quite as much as ignorance or lack of knowledge, than Plato can immediately make rejoinder that any choice we human beings make can only be a choice of what seems best to us at the moment. Hence if what seems best to us turns out to be not really best for us, then our choice will have been a bad one; but it will always ultimately be nothing but ignorance which is the cause of such bad choices, and so it can only be ignorance that is the ultimate cause of all of our failures.

6. A possible answer to Plato

Yet there is a weakness in this Platonic argument after all. For note that Plato's defense is ever to appeal to the principle that a man's choices can only be choices of what seems best to him at the moment. Nor can this principle be attacked, for it is not only true, but perhaps even a tautology since "to choose" simply means "to choose that which seems best." Still, this principle alone does not suffice to make good Plato's case. For not only must he show that our choices, when we make them, are determined by our opinions of what is best; he must also show that our opinions of what is best, when we have them, necessarily determine our choices. Nor do these two principles by any means come down to the same thing. For while it may be true that if and when I make a choice, I can only choose that which at the time seems best, it does not necessarily follow from this that if and when I have an opinion of what is best for me, I necessarily choose to act on this opinion.

However, it is precisely with reference to the latter situation that Aristotle's insistence upon the need for moral virtue, as distinct from intellectual virtue, is of particular pertinence. For Aristotle was not questioning the fact that we always make our choices on the basis of some sort of immediate opinion or judgment as to what is best for us. Rather what worried him was that all too frequently our better judgment does not seem to determine our choice. On the contrary, when actually we get around to making a choice, we often choose that which in a calmer moment we readily recognize to have been exceedingly foolish and unwise. Hence the need for moral virtue, in addition to intellectual virtue — moral virtue, that is to say, which will serve to bring our actual choices and preferences into line with what our better judgment tells us is the better course for us to follow.

Viewed in this light, Plato's principle begins to appear not so much true, as merely trivially true. For granted that at the moment of choosing I always do choose that which seems best to me just then, what does this prove? It certainly does not prove that I will necessarily go through with my choice. For it may well be that no sooner do I start to do so than I change my mind; some other course of action suggests itself to me as being far better; my earlier choice will then cease to be operative and will be replaced by a new and different choice in line with my new and different opinions. Even if one were to go along with Plato's view to the point of conceding that my judgments as to what is better or worse do, either all of the time or most of the time, determine my choices, there is nothing in this situation to guarantee any constancy to such judgments. Hence to conclude from this that virtue is simply a matter of knowledge would seem to be either trivial and insignificant, or else downright misleading and even mistaken.

To take a familiar, if trite, example, suppose that I well know that my irritability and bad temper are serious weaknesses in my character, leading me repeatedly to do things that are foolish and regrettable. No doubt this knowledge of my own weakness gives rise on my part to repeated firm resolves to try to correct my bad habits. But if a telephone call interrupts me as I am taking a nap, if a driver on the highway suddenly puts on the brakes without signalling, if a secretary fails to get the letter typed which I had said had to go out in the afternoon mail—then what happens? I blow my top; I forget all about those earlier sensible considerations as to how stupid such displays of temper are and what a serious reflection they are upon my character and personality.

And what about Plato? In one sense, he is not exactly refuted, for even in my fit of temper I do choose to act in accordance with what my judgment *at that moment* tells me is all right and what I should do. But in another sense he is completely refuted. Virtue is not simply a matter of knowledge; it is far more a matter of abiding by one's knowledge or remaining constant to it, instead of letting it be forever displaced by numberless counter-opinions and judgments that are determined by our passions and whims of the moment.

7. Implications with respect to human responsibility

After this rather long digression on Plato, we may be in a somewhat better position to understand the peculiar nature of human choice, and more specifically, just how and in what sense our bad choices are a cause of our human failures. There is also the question of our responsibility for such failures, once it be granted that these failures are due not so much to ignorance as to bad choices.

On this latter score it is interesting to note that if the "Platonic" theory (i.e., that interpretation and development of Plato's ideas that we have been presenting) were correct and if ignorance were the sole reason for our failures, then there would be no way in which we could be justly held responsible for our own failures. Quite the contrary, since on the Platonic view every human being always does the best he knows how; hence a man's not doing any better would be due simply to his not knowing any better. Nor could he be blamed for his ignorance, considering that, had he been able to find out what he needed to know, and had he realized how important it was to find out, he would certainly have done so. Accordingly, on any view which holds that virtue is but a matter of knowledge and vice one of ignorance, no man can very well be held personally responsible for being as he is.

On the other hand, once this Platonic theory is refuted and rejected, will it not be a different story as regards human responsibility? For now, although it must still be conceded that no man can choose any course of action other than that which seems best to him at the moment, still the mere fact that a certain course happens to seem best to him does not mean that he will necessarily choose it. On the contrary, it is always possible for him to change his opinion: he can think further about the matter and so come to realize that his original preference was unwise; or he can simply let himself be cajoled into thinking otherwise under the influence of a change of feeling or mood. For that matter, even his original opinion of the situation might well have been a different one. After all, it is a simple fact borne in upon us repeatedly that even though at a given moment things do appear to us as they do, still they might not have seemed that way at all, had we but chosen to look farther, or had we taken pains to investigate more carefully; or contrariwise, had we not bestirred ourselves to see what we did see, or had we not taken the trouble to inform ourselves as we did.

8. *Human responsibility as involving human freedom*

Just what are we to understand by this expression "it is always possible" for us to change our opinions as to what is better or worse for us, or to have reached a different opinion in the first place? What is involved here is not merely a logical possibility, or even a mere physical possibility, in the sense that the various external causes and factors productive of my opinions might have been different or might still become different, thus causing my opinions either to have been or to be other than what they are. What is meant here is a possibility that is open to me in the sense of being within my own power and disposition. Thus when I say, "I should never have done that, if only I had stopped to think," or "I knew what a foolish thing that was to do; why then did I let my temper get the better of me?"—in all such cases the implication is not merely that the results would have been different, had the circumstances been different, but also that it was somehow due to me that the circumstances were not different: I could have changed them, but I didn't. Thus the responsibility for the final result rests with me.

You might reply, "It is true that we often speak this way about ourselves, as if it were within our power to have acted differently from the way we did. But is this any more than just a common way of speaking? What exactly does it mean? Does it not call up all the problems connected with free will, a notion which in the final analysis reduces to sheer unintelligibility?"

A. VALUE JUDGMENTS AS FREE JUDGMENTS

Thus far we have avoided use of the term "free will," because of the many difficulties connected with this expression. But perhaps we can avoid its use no longer. Or maybe for our purposes the Scholastic term, *liberum arbitrium,* "free choice" or perhaps even "free judgment," would be better. In any case, despite the difficulties that arise in using such notions, we believe that they can be rendered meaningful and intelligible. In explaining them, we propose to follow, for the most part, an explanation that has become traditional in Western philosophy. It runs something like this.

There is a certain sense in which we human beings never seem satisfied with anything. Whatever it is that a man possesses, wealth or learning or fame or competence or even a beautiful woman, he can always think of something else that he still does not have and that he wants. The reason for this insatiability in the demands and desires of human nature is that man is a being who can form what we might call the notion of an absolute and infinite good. True, most of us in our daily lives don't go around talking about the "infinite good." Nor is it anything that we can actually point to, being a purely abstract notion, or perhaps better, a notion that forever transcends anything that we come upon in concrete experience. But however little we may talk about it, our conduct and behavior are not infrequently dominated by the notion of it—witness our restlessness, our striving, our boredom and dissatisfaction with what we have, our ever recurrent pursuit of the novel and the different. One could almost say that the very logic of our human situation makes this sort of tension and dissatisfaction almost inevitable. For whatever it is that I am, or whatever it is that I have, in the very nature of the case there is bound to be something else that I am not, or that I do not have. What's more, as an intelligent being, I can scarcely avoid realizing that in being or having anything, there are countless other things that in the very nature of the case I must do without.

Little wonder, then, that such being our human condition, our choices will never be absolutely determined by any one opinion as to what is better or worse for ourselves. For no sooner will one course of action appear to be the best one open to us than the limitations of such a course will begin to impress themselves upon us: if we follow this particular course, we shall be unable to do certain other things that begin to appear attractive—we shall be deprived of this, barred from that, deflected from something else. Under a bombardment of such considerations, our original judgment as to what was best for us may change completely; something else may begin to appear more to our liking.

Moreover, the ironical thing is that this freedom of judgment, or freedom of will, operates even with respect to those things which really are best for us, and not only with respect to those which only seem to be so. For example, as regards the examined life itself, it makes no difference how clearly I may recognize its superior claims or how convinced I may be that it is the only life for me, still it is a way of life which is certainly limited when compared with the abstract standard of the infinite good. In consequence, my judgment that it is the best life for me, however true it may be, is still not a necessarily determined judgment. On the contrary. I can hardly fail to recognize that in order to be a Socrates, say, I shall have to give up a lot of things that may be very dear to me—comforts and luxuries, or place and position, or wealth, or even my career as scholar or general or diplomat or scientist; I might even have to drink the hemlock! When the realization of such sacrifices is borne in upon me, it would hardly surprise anyone if I were to begin to feel that the examined life really didn't have so much to recommend it after all—despite the fact that in truth it might still be the best life for me and indeed for any man.

We are now in a position to discern the real meaning of these notions of free will and free judgments. Free judgment means no more than that in matters pertaining to what is of value for us and what it is best for us to do, our judgment is never necessarily determined to any one opinion alone. Even if our opinion happens to be a true opinion and we know it to be true, that opinion still does not necessarily determine our course of action. For compared with the abstract notion of an absolute or infinite good, any concrete notion of what is good for us here and now will inevitably appear restricted. Hence as we consider all that we shall not be getting, all that we shall be giving up and sacrificing, if we act upon our present judgment, it is not surprising that our judgment itself may change and that what had formerly seemed so attractive and worth while may now appear less so.

B. FREE JUDGMENTS AND FREE CHOICES

Nevertheless, this notion of "free judgment" cannot be properly understood save in close connection with the correlative notion of "free will" or "free choice." To be sure, a judgment, even though it be a judgment of value, is nevertheless a proper judgment. That is to say, in any judgment of value, we do in a sense judge that something is the case, e.g., that a certain course of action is the best one to follow under the circumstances. And being a judgment, this will be either true or false. At the same time, this is the sort of judgment that can only be a contingent truth, not a necessary truth: it is something which, even though it be true, might conceivably have been otherwise. For example, suppose I make the statement: "At this hour, 10:30 P.M., on this day, March 24, 1962, I am sitting at my desk writing." This statement is in fact true; and yet it is perfectly conceivable that it might not have been so: instead of being at my desk I might, alas, have been sound asleep in bed, or drinking a glass of beer with a friend, or reading a good book.

In this sense, then, an ordinary judgment of value is no more than a contingent truth: it could be true, but it need not be. Nevertheless, in holding these judgments of value to be free judgments more is meant than merely that they are contingent. For in addition to being contingent, such judgments of value are implied instructions or commands —commands to ourselves to choose to act in accordance with what we have judged to be the better course. Nevertheless, since as human beings we can scarcely avoid measuring our judgments of value against an ultimate and abstract standard of infinite good or absolute value, and since such a comparison always reveals the limited and restrictive character of the value that is being prescribed for us, it is inevitable that the implied directive or command that is involved in our judgment will not necessarily move us to act. On the contrary, we are always free to choose not to act. In other words, the "freedom" of such a judgment of value must be understood with reference to the freedom of choice which that judgment leaves, so to speak, undetermined and unnecessitated.

But further, the freedom that is involved in free will and free choice must also be understood with reference to a certain freedom that is involved in what we have called a free judgment in regard to values. As we have already seen in our discussion of Plato, a choice can only be of that which seems best to us at the moment. In this sense any human choice always presupposes a judgment of value as a sort of guide or directive. When we say that any of our finite human judgments of value always leaves us free to choose otherwise, this can only mean that other and alternative judgments of value must lie ready at hand, in accordance with which we may make a different choice. Not only that, but our very dissatisfaction, or at least our feeling that we are not entirely satisfied, with the limited and restricted values that are being recommended to us creates a demand for new and different directives, i.e., for other and alternative judgments of value. This is why, we would suggest, our very judgments themselves appear to be not so much determined by the facts, as elicited by our needs and wants. In this sense, they appear to be free and at our disposal. And so, we should be able to understand a little more clearly what is meant by human freedom. In contrast to all other instances of appetite, impulse, tendency, tropism, etc., such as occur throughout the rest of nature, the values that elicit our distinctively human choices and preferences are never uniquely determining. Instead, being subject to comparison with a standard of absolute value, such values always leave us free to choose something else; that is to say, we find ourselves, with respect to the objects of our wishes and desires, always caught up in an interplay of free judgment and free choice of the sort we have just been describing.

But, of course, where there is freedom, there is responsibility. Indeed, this is the sense of those locutions and turns of phrase which are the common coin of our daily lives and which no amount of philosophical sophistication can ever enable us to dispense with: "I chose to do this, but I didn't have to, I could have chosen otherwise"; "I decided on this course of action because at the time it seemed best to me; but if only I had stopped to think, I should have realized how foolish the whole thing was"; etc.

More generally, however, where this matter of human responsibility is impressed upon us, and even sometimes overwhelms us, it is in connection with the good life as a whole. What human perfection consists in, what true human happiness involves, is in one sense determined by human nature itself; but it is not determined at all that we shall actually live this way. On the contrary, we ourselves must choose to do so. Moreover, we have to choose such a mode of life in the face of the fact that in comparison with an absolute good, it can appear distressingly limited and lacking in all sorts of things that we might wish for. But it is still the best life for us. We are all capable of recognizing this; indeed, we all, in a sense, do recognize it. And yet how few of us earnestly seek to attain it, to say nothing of actually succeeding. Here is where we do seem to be without excuse. It is not because of ignorance that we fail, ultimately, it is because we don't choose when we could choose. In this sense, there is no one and no thing that we can ultimately hold responsible for such failure, save only ourselves.

6

Bad Luck and the Force of Circumstances as the Causes of Failure

*1. But how can we be blamed when it is
not we who make ourselves what we are?*

But is not all this talk about how our bad choices or our not know-ing any better may be causes of our failure and unhappiness—is not all this wide of the mark? To be sure, few of us perhaps are truly happy, and many of us do not make much of a "go" of our lives. But isn't this because of the countless adverse circumstances that beset any human being throughout the course of his life—all of us some of the time and some of us all of the time? Such circumstances are not of our own choosing, certainly not of our own creation. We just find ourselves pursued and engulfed by them, and there is nothing we can do about it. A human being cannot live his life in a test-tube—and even if he could his condition would not be one of his own making, but one that was made for him. All of us, as soon as we begin to reflect and to ex-amine our lives, find ourselves already plunged *in medias res.* Things, people, influences, circumstances, environment, conditions of life, heredity, and a thousand and one other factors have already made us what we are.

What is more, our earlier analogy between the life of man and the life of an acorn reinforces the point that our so-called success or fail-ure in life is not, strictly speaking, our own doing, but rather some-thing that is done for us, or better, to us. Nobody holds the acorn "re-sponsible" for either succeeding or failing to grow into an oak. If the conditions are right, the acorn will develop and mature automatically; and if not, not. Likewise, one might argue, if there is such a thing as human nature, which predisposes every man to develop toward perfection, whether a given individual actually attains such perfection will depend not on him, but on circumstances. The attainment of such perfection may depend upon having the right knowledge and making the right choices, but given favorable circumstances of life, such knowledge and such choices will be forthcoming automatically; if circumstances are unfavorable, they will not. In the final analysis, human success or failure seems to be little more than a matter of good luck or bad luck, for which we ourselves cannot be held accountable.

2. The issue of scientific determinism—an ethical red herring?

In confirmation of the view that there is no such thing as personal moral responsibility for one's actions, one has only to shift from a commonsense context to the perspective of contemporary science. Generally speaking, in modern psychology and sociology, to say nothing of physiology and biology, notions like "free will" and "personal responsibility" are not employed at all; they make no sense in the context of a scientific explanation. Nor is this surprising. For while the older schemes of a rigorous, mechanistic determinism may not be compatible with many of the recent developments in quantum physics, we are still not justified in reintroducing concepts like "freedom" and "moral responsibility" into the scientific domain.

On the contrary, the basic schema of explanation that continues to be almost the exclusive resource of all the different sciences in the contemporary world is a simple device of functional correlation. Events or phenomena of type A are correlated with certain other events of type B, so that the occurrence of an A is taken to be simply a function of B. For example, the stimulus-response scheme in modern psychology operates in this way: the response of the organism is treated as a mere function of the stimulus plus a certain initial state of the organism at the time of the stimulus. In the context of such an explanatory scheme there does not seem to be the slightest need for the more usual, commonsense, "anthropomorphic" type of explanation, according to which an animal or a human being sees or recognizes something as valuable and in consequence comes to want it and choose it.

With his usual clarity, Bertrand Russell explains how one can transplant or transpose oneself from one's commonsense, everyday way of regarding things into the scientific perspective of modern psychology:

> We all think that, by watching the behaviour of animals, we can discover more or less what they desire. If this is the case—and I fully agree that it is—desire must be capable of being exhibited in actions, for it is only the actions of animals that we can observe. They *may* have minds in which all sorts of things take place, but we can know nothing about their minds except by means of inferences from their actions; and the more such inferences are examined, the more dubious they appear. It would seem, therefore, that actions alone must be the test of the desires of animals. From this it is an easy step to the conclusion that an animal's desire is nothing but a characteristic of a certain series of actions, namely, those which would be commonly regarded as inspired by the desire in question. And when it has been shown that this view affords a satisfactory account of animal desires, it is not difficult to see that the same explanation is applicable to the desires of human beings.
>
> We judge easily from the behaviour of an animal of a familiar kind whether it is hungry or thirsty, or pleased or displeased, or inquisitive or terrified. The verification of our judgment, so far as verification is possible, must be derived from the immediately succeeding actions of the animal. Most people would say that they infer first something about the animal's state of mind—whether it is hungry or thirsty and so on—and thence derive their expectations as to its subsequent conduct. But this detour through the animal's supposed mind is wholly unnecessary. We can say simply: The animal's behaviour during the last minute has had those characteristics which distinguish what is called "hunger," and it is likely that its actions during the next minute will be similar in this respect, unless it finds food, or is interrupted by a stronger impulse, such as fear. An animal which is hungry is restless, it goes to the places where food is often to be found, it sniffs with its nose or peers with its

eyes or otherwise increases the sensitiveness of its sense-organs; as soon as it is near enough to food for its sense-organs to be affected, it goes to it with all speed and proceeds to eat; after which, if the quantity of food has been sufficient, its whole demeanour changes: it may very likely lie down and go to sleep. These things and others like them are observable phenomena distinguishing a hungry animal from one which is not hungry. The characteristic mark by which we recognize a series of actions which display hunger is not the animal's mental state, which we cannot observe, but something in its bodily behaviour; it is this observable trait in the bodily behaviour that I am proposing to call "hunger," not some possibly mythical and certainly unknowable ingredient of the animal's mind.[1]

For our present purposes, we might note one sentence in particular in this quotation from Russell: "And when it has been shown that this view affords a satisfactory account of animal desires, it is not difficult to see that the same explanation is applicable to the desires of human beings." Indeed, it is just this sort of explanation that modern psychologists do employ with reference to human behavior; and it is profitably employed, for on the basis of such a scheme, the behavior of human beings, both individually and in groups, can be predicted with remarkable success.

Such a mode of explanation and prediction enables the psychologist to dispense altogether with the entire paraphernalia that we have been using thus far in our discussion of human moral conduct, that is, the notions of human understanding and of human choice based on such understanding, in other words, of intellectual virtue and of moral virtue. The implications of such scientific behaviorism, or determinism, for questions of human responsibility are perfectly clear. On such a view, there is no such thing as human responsibility or accountability, for such ideas are unnecessary and irrelevant to the explanation of human behavior.

There is an interesting parallel here with Plato's theory that virtue is merely a matter of knowledge, and vice of ignorance. In the Platonic view, if a man knows what is best for him he will automatically do what is best for him; if he doesn't he won't. He himself has no control over whether or not he possesses such knowledge. Similarly on the scientific, deterministic view of human nature, given a certain stimulus, it can be predicted that a given organism will respond in a certain way. The organism itself has no control over the way it responds to stimuli, or over what stimuli are presented to it. On neither view can an individual be held accountable for his own behavior, since in neither case can the individual exert any influence over his own actions or even over his own choices.

But if there is to be any such thing as ethics, there must be such a thing as personal responsibility. And if there is to be personal responsibility, then one must maintain the claims of something like free choice as a cause of human behavior, against the Platonist claim that knowledge is the exclusive determinant of such behavior, and against the determinists' claim that external factors are the sole causes.

In undertaking a refutation of determinism, we might as well start by quoting Dr. Johnson: "Sir, all theory is against the freedom of the will; all experience for it."[2] However irritated one may be by Johnson's dogmatism, one must be impressed by his appeal to experience. For scientific determinism is, after all, only the product of a philosophic theory which is controverted at almost every step by our own unsophisticated, but inescapable, everyday human experience. We may even suggest that determinism is the sort of thing that is defensible only in theory but not in practice.

Nor is this contention based simply on the fact that in our everyday experience we do seem to be free, we do think and feel as if we had freedom of choice, no matter how convinced we may have become intellectually that our behavior is completely determined by forces outside our control. In addition, we would suggest that the determinist can scarcely avoid falling into a kind of practical inconsistency that is not unlike the inconsistency of which we found the relativist to be guilty. To see how this must be so, let us try to project ourselves imaginatively into the experience of a man who is a determinist by conviction.

Such a man must be convinced that men's actions and behavior do not proceed from anything like knowledge and understanding or from choices based on such knowledge. But what of his own choices? As we have seen, any human choice necessarily implies some judgment of value, some judgment to the effect that one course of action is preferable to another. But if one is a determinist, what implications will his determinism have for his own judgments of value?

However the determinist may answer this question, he cannot avoid being inconsistent with his own principles. For whatever the implications of determinism may be with respect to our judgments of value, the very fact that determinism is acknowledged to have such implications at all is sufficient to refute that determinism. Have we not seen that it is a part of what one means by determinism to suppose that our conduct and behavior do not proceed from anything like knowledge or opinions about our human situation or from choices based on such opinions? And yet if our judgments of value are admitted to be somehow affected by our deterministic convictions, in the sense that the former tend to be either upset or confirmed or at least in some way influenced by the latter, then it would seem that we do make choices based on judgments of value which in turn are based on such knowledge and opinions as we happen to have regarding ourselves and the world round about us.

On the other hand, if the determinist, wishing to escape these consequences, turns to the other alternative of supposing that his deterministic theories and convictions have absolutely no effect on his judgments of value, then he must find himself in an even less defensible position. For how can a man be convinced of something without being critical of, perhaps even looking down his nose at, those who are not so convinced or who are of a contrary opinion? Indeed, the behavioristic psychologist—to select him by way of example—is not noted for lacking confidence that he is right. In fact, to be firmly convinced of anything is inevitably to adopt a mode of behavior that implies that one thinks one's opponents are mistaken, if not foolish.

In other words, so far as one's own self is concerned, and one's own behavior, there is no way that any man—even a determinist—can totally isolate his personal choices and preferences from his convictions as to what is so. It is true that when a scientist, or a psychologist, or an old-fashioned determinist in philosophy, looks at his neighbor, or his academic colleagues, or his own wife and child, he could consistently treat them as if they were just so many puppets or automata whom he, the expert, can manipulate and condition much as one does monkeys, rats, and guinea pigs. But that he should bring himself under the same deterministic principles that he applies to other men—this, we would suggest, is simply impossible without falling into the most glaring practical inconsistency.

3. The force of circumstances: does it determine us or only challenge us?

However easy it may be to expose the inconsistencies of various theories of determinism, we can scarcely blink the facts of life so completely as not to recognize that there are countless determining factors that operate to make us what we are, and to make us happy or miserable. Indeed, one might be tempted to revive once more the idea that we have already tried to lay to rest, the idea that morality, or living one's life successfully and well, is nothing but a matter of art, of skill and cleverness, of mere intellectual virtue.

If we suppose that living well is only a matter of possessing certain favorable opportunities, plus the wit to exploit them, then the whole thing is pretty much a matter of luck. If I had died in infancy, one could scarcely say that I had had sufficient opportunity to attain my natural human perfection. Or if I survived, but with an I.Q. of a moron, I could hardly be expected to achieve much in the way of human perfection either. We cannot doubt that the circumstances of human life vary greatly, ranging from the most favorable to the most unfavorable. Not infrequently, they are such as to make perfection in anything like the sense in which we have defined it simply impossible; but for these circumstances we ourselves cannot be held responsible.

Nevertheless, for most of us, most of the time, our adversities and ill fortune are not such as to leave us completely without resource. Nor is such resource exclusively an intellectual affair. Quite the contrary. Suppose I find myself unjustly thrown into prison, or suppose I suddenly lose my financial independence and am reduced to the most severe penury and want. Under such circumstances some people, no doubt, might behave much more cleverly than I: they might figure out ways to escape from prison, or they might devise some ingenious means of recouping their financial losses. But this kind of intellectual ingenuity is not of primary moment in a moral context. From the moral standpoint the important thing is not whether I am shrewd enough to avoid certain misfortunes, or to extricate myself from them once they have befallen me, but whether I have sufficient character (moral virtue) to sustain them in such a way as a good man or a wise man would do. For imprisonment and financial ruin are misfortunes which may be borne either nobly or ignobly. Which way, then, shall I bear them?

More generally, is not much of the adversity which afflicts human beings of a sort to leave us with considerable choice as to how we shall respond and adjust to it—patiently or like spoiled children; like "good sports" or bad sports; bravely or ignominiously; maintaining our sense of justice and balance, or giving way to meanness and vindictiveness? And what holds in ill fortune is equally true as regards good fortune. Few of us are such thoroughgoing philosophers that we would not like to wake up some fine morning to find that we had fallen heir to a million dollars. But are we sure that we would not let such good fortune go to our heads? How do we know that, far from behaving wisely and intelligently, we might prove to be just as big a fool as the next man?

Of course, it is hardly likely that such somber philosophical reflections will dissuade many of us from dreaming now and then of what we might do "with a little bit, with a little bit, with a little bit of bloomin' luck." Nor is there any reason why they should; for what's wrong with having a little bit of luck? Nothing at all. But the important thing is how we take our good fortune, or our ill fortune. That is what determines whether we are well off or not, not the good or ill fortune itself.

In other words, so long as the circumstances of our lives and the changes and chances of fortune leave us with at least some freedom of choice or of judgment as to how we shall act in the face of what has befallen us, then our fate as wise men or as fools will still be largely in our own hands. Our success or failure will not be due simply to the force of circumstances, but to our own character and our own exercise of moral virtue.

4. The moral problem transposed into a legal context by way of illustration

Lest all this seem a bit implausible and far-fetched, let us once more shift the discussion to the context of criminal law. Just as earlier in regard to the question of our responsibility for ignorance, so now in regard to the question of the extent to which the mere force of circumstances determines our well-being, it may prove instructive to consider how the principles that are operative in the criminal law are analogous to, and hence illustrate, the principles that are relevant in the sphere of morals and ethics. In criminal law the question is usually a fairly straightforward one of a man's responsibility for the infliction of certain legally defined harms; more specifically, in the present connection, it would be a question of a person's responsibility for harms which he had inflicted when, in fact, he had been in some way coerced into doing what he did.

If in a given instance it could be shown that the accused had really been compelled to do something, in the sense that he quite literally had no choice at all but to do it, then clearly in the eyes of the law he would not be held responsible for his action. For instance, if despite my violent resistance a group of thugs should overpower me, force a gun into my hand, and then move my finger so as to pull the trigger and cause the gun to go off, I could scarcely be held responsible for any injuries that the shot might cause to someone else.

Nevertheless, most cases involving necessity or compulsion are not as clear-cut as this. If they were, they would probably never even have been prosecuted. The more usual situation is one in which the agent is subjected to pressures which are beyond his control, but in the face of which he is still left with certain alternatives as to how he shall react in the face of these circumstances. For instance, consider the following summary account of a variety of particular cases, quoted from a textbook by a distinguished contemporary authority on criminal law:

> Thus, if a ship is cast by a storm upon a shore, the entry is not illegal; hence a passenger on the boat, deported from the country, is not guilty of illegal re-entry in such a case. So, also, as to failure to be present at a required time and place (*e.g.*, a juror, witness,

or soldier on leave) because of a flood or a broken bridge, or any other physical force that makes locomotion impossible. If a juror or witness has been imprisoned, the fact that a human agency created the barriers makes such cases no less instances of physical causation so far as the above persons are concerned, *e.g.,* a cafe owner whose establishment remained open beyond the fixed closing time because he was tied hand and foot by his patrons. Thus, also, a married woman who was raped did not commit adultery, according to Ulpian. Where automobile lights are put out by an electric storm, this does not constitute a violation of the ordinance requiring them. But a beach-bather whose clothes were stolen can not plead physical necessity to a charge of nudeness since he had the alternative of remaining in the water until relieved.[3]

The solemnity with which these cases are reviewed may be amusing, but the principle that seems to govern in these weighty judicial decisions regarding nude beach-bathers, raped matrons, and resistant café owners is not unlike the principle that would presumably govern in cases of comparable moral or ethical judgments.

The relevant question is always, first, whether the circumstances were such as to leave the agent any choice, and second, whether, granted that he did have a certain choice, he made the choice that a reasonable man, or a morally good man, might be expected to make in such circumstances.

To take another classical example from the law, what about jettisoning a ship's cargo in order to save the lives of the passengers? Obviously, for a ship's officer to jettison a cargo when there was no necessity for his doing so would be a criminal act. On the other hand, when in the case of a severe storm at sea it really did become necessary to jettison the cargo, just what does "necessary" mean here? Clearly, it is not an absolute necessity: the officer could always have chosen not to throw the cargo overboard; but had he so chosen he would have endangered the whole ship and the lives of the crew and the passengers. In other words, what is involved here is not the sort of necessity that excludes human choice altogether, but rather the sort of necessity that comes into play when we have to choose between the lesser of two evils.

As the older moralists would say, acts of the sort here under consideration are "mixed acts," i.e., acts which we do choose to perform, but which we choose not because we prefer them in themselves, but because no better alternative seems open to us. Moreover, so long as any choice is open to us at all, then it would seem that whether in a moral or merely a legal context, our choice is one for which we may properly be held responsible.

5. Back from law to ethics again

Once more let us see how this principle works out in terms of a specific legal or moral situation. Quoting again from the same legal authority:

> The leading decision in this country on the defence of necessity is U.S. v. Holmes. The case is especially significant because it is unexcelled in its suggestiveness of the quality of action taken in "states of necessity."
>
> In March of 1841 the American ship, *William Brown,* sailed from Liverpool, carrying a crew of seventeen, and sixty-five emigrants bound for the United States. On April 19th, after thirty-eight days at sea, it struck an iceberg late at night and began to fill rapidly. Thirty-two passengers, the first mate and eight seamen got into a "long-boat"; the captain, eight seamen and one passenger took to the smaller "jollyboat." In little more than an hour the *William Brown* sank, carrying with her thirty-one passengers, the majority of them, children. "But not one of the officers or crew went down with the ship." The two lifeboats parted the next morning, when it was apparent that the long-boat would be unmanageable, indeed, the first mate had already informed the captain that "it would be necessary to cast lots and throw some overboard." "Let it be the last resort," said the captain, ordering his crew to pull away. Almost immediately after being occupied, the long-boat had begun to take water through a plugged hole that became loosened. The boat was so crowded that the passengers were lying and sitting on one another; there was not sufficient room to bail out the water quickly. For

twenty-four hours they carried on in the icy waters off the coast of Labrador. Then it began to rain and it rained all the next day, and by night the sea had become very rough and the wind stronger than ever. The men bailed frantically but the boat seemed doomed. A woman passenger, immersed in water almost to her knees, heard someone cry, "we are sinking," and said, "we shall all be lost." Another shouted: "The plug is out. The boat is sinking. God have mercy on our poor souls." The mate gave the order to cast overboard all the male passengers except two whose wives were present. Unheeded, he repeated the order; then, fourteen men were thrown overboard, and two young women, sisters of one of them, either met a like fate or chose to join their brother. The next morning two other men who had hidden themselves were discovered, and the crew put both of them overboard. Almost immediately afterwards the longboat was sighted by the *Crescent;* all survivors were transferred to it, and later disembarked at Le Havre.[4]

In trying to assess either the moral or the legal responsibility of the first mate for the deaths of the men thrown overboard, the problem becomes one primarily of fixing the kind or degree of "necessity" under which the mate acted. The man could certainly say in his own defense, and others could say on his behalf, that he did "nothing but what inexorable necessity demanded," that he did not want to cause the deaths of the men who were thrown overboard, but that he had to, circumstances having made it necessary.

One immediately recognizes that there was no absolute necessity involved here: it was only in consequence of the mate's own decision that the men were sent to their deaths, and he could have chosen otherwise. It was thus one of those "mixed acts," in which the action did proceed from the agent's own choice, albeit a choice which did not commend itself to him in itself, but only as the lesser of two evils. Nevertheless, since the action was one which the agent did choose and decide upon himself, it was one for which he was himself responsible. Accordingly, putting aside the strictly legal question of guilt or innocence, and confining our attention to the moral question alone, what is to be said for the mate's choice in such a case? Was it the right choice?

Was it a choice that a good man or wise man would have made in similar circumstances?

To judge from the somewhat scant details which are given in the summary of the case, it would hardly seem that the first mate acted in a particularly heroic or even morally commendable fashion. There is even a suggestion that he shared with the captain the blame for themselves taking to the lifeboats and trying to save their own skins, even though many of the passengers were left aboard and went down with the ship. One would hardly say that the mate's decisions and actions reflected any very remarkable display of moral virtue—of courage, of dignity, of sense of responsibility, of greatness of soul.

Nevertheless, for our present purposes, the more interesting question is not whether the mate proved under the circumstances to be a man of somewhat questionable moral stature. Rather I suggest that we pose the question a little differently: suppose we ask how a man of unquestioned moral stature would have acted under the same circumstances. What would he have done? Suppose Socrates himself were in the shoes of the first mate, and suppose that he had made his choice, exercising the relevant intellectual and moral virtues, what would his decision have been? Strangely enough, his decision might very well have been the same as the first mate's.

It is quite conceivable that a man in complete possession of himself, sensing fully his responsibilities in the situation, not for a moment thinking simply of saving himself, but being quite ready to sacrifice his own life first if need be, might nevertheless decide that in these particular circumstances the proper course was for him to sacrifice the lives of some of the passengers first. He might realize that only a very skillful seaman could keep the longboat afloat at all; that only an officer with sufficient authority could keep the distraught passengers, to say nothing of the cowardly and irresponsible members of the crew, in line. Hence it is readily imaginable that reluctantly, and doubtless even with many misgivings, our Socrates, turned ship's officer, might have made the same choice as the rather shabby-seeming first mate: the one, quite as much as the other, might have given the order to have some of the passengers thrown overboard in order to save the lives of the others.

A. DO WE FIND OURSELVES COMMITTED TO A
MERE ETHICS OF GOOD INTENTIONS AFTER ALL?

But does this not point up a curious paradox, perhaps even a glaring weakness, in the whole ethical theory we have thus far been expounding? If our hypothetical Socrates in the role of first mate did what he did, exercising the moral virtues, then by our account his conduct would be morally commendable and right. On the other hand, the actual first mate doing the same thing, not from moral virtue, but irresponsibly and primarily in order to save his own skin—in his case the very same conduct would have to be adjudged reprehensible and bad. Would it not seem, then, that on our view of ethics, it makes not the slightest difference what a man does; it is only how he does it that counts—i.e., in what spirit he does it, and whether he does it with good will or not? In short, the ethics of the examined life, of the intelligent life, turns out to be no more than an ethics of good intentions. Or does it?

Before answering this question, let us consider still another implication of the way in which we have been suggesting that one assess the moral worth of actions performed under so-called necessity. To recur once more to the sinking of the *William Brown,* it is conceivable that not every good man, finding himself in the shoes of the first mate, would have decided to do what the first mate did. Socrates might have decided to throw some of the passengers overboard, but it is also conceivable that he might have come to a very different decision. He might have reasoned in some such way as this: "It's true that my skill and my authority are probably necessary to keep the longboat afloat; hence if I sacrificed myself, the rest are much more likely to perish. On the other hand, as a ship's officer, it is my responsibility to subordinate my own welfare to that of the passengers and the ship as a whole; not only that, but as a human being I realize that it is hardly the part of a brave man, to say nothing of a man with a sense of his own dignity and responsibility, to try to work things around in such a way that it is his own life that is saved, while others are sacrificed. What's more, even though it might well seem in this particular case as if duty prescribed the same course of action as that dictated by self-interest, still such a seeming coincidence of duty and self-interest is always to be regarded with suspicion: it is only too likely that in such circumstances one's sup-posedly reasoned judgment of what one's duty is will in fact be merely a cowardly rationalization. Consequently, all things considered, it would seem to be the better part for me to throw myself overboard first. In this way I can make sure that I keep my own slate clean; and in addi-tion, it might possibly serve as an example to others, encouraging and even inspiring them to take themselves in hand, and overcome their panic, and act somewhat more like sane and sensible human beings."

Accepting such a line of reasoning as sound and defensible, the con-clusion from our example seems clear: two morally good men, when confronted with the same circumstances, might well decide that the situation called for radically different types of conduct, and both de-cisions would be entirely warranted and morally commendable. More-over, this conclusion tends to reinforce and confirm the earlier hy-pothesis which we considered above, viz., that in response to a given situation the same course of action would have to be adjudged morally right and commendable when performed by a good man, and not so when performed by a man who was not good. In both instances, it would seem that it is not the act itself that counts, but only the inten-tions of the actor or agent. In other words, what we have here does seem to be an ethics of good intentions.

B. BUT THE GOOD LIFE MUST BE AN INTELLIGENT LIFE, NOT JUST A WELL-MEANING LIFE

Not entirely so, however. It is true that if the goal of our ethical en-deavors is nothing less than the achievement of an examined life, then we are concerned to judge not the isolated act, or even the effects of such an act upon others and upon society; rather it is the human being himself that we are trying to judge.

"Oh," you will say, "this is only to push the issue one step further back. For what is it that makes a man a good man, on the theory here expounded, if it be not simply his being well-meaning or well-inten-tioned? It's not what he does that counts so much as the quality of his choices. It's not even what the man knows that seems to count. For ultimately the quality of his choices is determined not so much by the shrewdness that he displays in making them as by the moral virtue that he exercises. Does this give the lie to the whole idea of the good life being the intelligent life? Intelligence seems to be largely irrelevant: you might be a perfect ass, but so long as you meant well, you would at least be entitled to the distinction of being good, for whatever that might be worth!"

This criticism misses the mark, though, in its equation of moral virtue with mere good intentions. For as we have already seen, moral virtue is not something that functions independently of knowledge and intelligence; on the contrary, the moral virtues are nothing but habits or dispositions to choose in accordance with our intelligence and our better judgment. Yet the kind of judgment that is relevant here is not judgment about how best to win wars, avoid depressions, or retire early and live longer. It is the kind of intelligent judgment that is concerned simply with oneself and with what it takes to be a truly human being. Without this knowledge, not all the good intentions in the world will serve to make one's actions the actions of a good man. And with such understanding, one still needs the so-called moral virtues in order that he will actually want and come to choose those actions which are requisite in an intelligent, examined life.

Coming back to the main theme of the present section, it should now be clear that it is not the force of circumstances or the chances of fortune that ultimately make us well off or badly off. So long as the events which befall us leave us with any choice at all as to how we shall react to our fate, we then have the opportunity of reacting either in the way that a good man or a wise man would react, or otherwise. Thus our well-being still seems to remain pretty much in our own hands and to be our own responsibility.

6. A final doubt as to our freedom and responsibility in the face of adverse circumstances

All the same, we must not let ourselves be carried away by our own eloquence on the subject of man's freedom in the face of compelling circumstances and his responsibility for his own decisions and choices. Indeed, there is something disingenuous, not to say pharisaic, about our whole discussion of the tragedy of the *William Brown*. It is easy

enough to sit comfortably in one's study and write pompously and judi-
ciously about how the first mate failed to display the requisite moral
virtue in the situation in which he found himself. But suppose we ourselves had been out in the longboat in the icy waters of the Atlantic,
realizing that the boat was shipping water faster than it could be bailed
out, listening to the screams and shrieks of the desperate passengers,
knowing that the prospects of rescue were so slight as to be almost
non-existent, just how would we have conducted ourselves? Is it not
likely that we should have been, if anything, even less brave and less
heroic than the first mate? How then can we be so glib in our con-
demnation of him? And just how meaningful is it to say that the mate,
strictly speaking, was not forced to act as he did, that he could have
behaved otherwise?

In like manner, one could say that the American soldiers who were
captured in Korea, and who were subjected to weeks and weeks of
constant pressure and torture and brain-washing—one could say, of
course, that these men did not have to give in, that they could have
resisted the pressures exerted upon them, and that they were therefore responsible for any moral weaknesses that any of them may have
shown in the course of their ordeal. Or, to change the example, is there
any sense in saying that a person brought up in a totalitarian regime,
and conditioned from infancy to believe all the outpourings of party
propaganda and to manifest all the hatred and fanaticism that such
propaganda is meant to evoke—is there any sense in saying that such
a person nevertheless remains free not to be taken in by such lies and
that he is therefore responsible for not having tried to practice a more
examined life?

Certainly, warnings against self-righteousness and a holier-than-
thou attitude are entirely justified. Moreover, there is always a point
where external pressures become so compelling that their victim is left
with no freedom of choice at all. Our example of this was the man who
was completely overpowered and literally forced to pull the trigger of
a gun. One could also cite examples of where this point was reached,
when the pressures exerted were not merely crude physical pressures
but psychological ones.

It may be difficult, if not impossible, in practice to determine exactly
when this point is reached in the case of a given individual. Hence

one can never be sure just when a man's freedom of choice, and hence his responsibility for his actions, disappear entirely. Nevertheless, even long before any such end point is reached, it is obvious that the external forces exerted upon an individual may become so great that even though in the literal sense he may be said still to have some freedom of choice, for all practical purposes we recognize that the pressures on him were so great that we could not blame the man for acting as he did under the circumstances.

But even though charity and understanding are always in order in our assessment of the shortcomings of others, at the same time it is important that we ourselves not lose sight of the fact that, until that end point of what might be called absolute compulsion is reached, any human being, ourselves included, still has some slight freedom of choice left and thus remains fundamentally a responsible human being. This simple fact may be a source of no little uneasiness to us; it may even be a source of what the existentialists are wont to call dread or anxiety. For such a responsibility is very hard to live up to. Yet at the same time it is the ultimate source of our dignity as human beings, and hence of any hope that we may cherish for ourselves and our future.

7. Still one more doubt, this time concerning happiness: is the good life necessarily the happy life?

And now for one last point that may have seemed particularly implausible and unrealistic in the foregoing account of man's comparative independence of the changes and chances of fortune. We have argued that no matter what happens to a man, so long as he has any freedom of choice left at all, he will continue to have the option of re-acting to his fate in the way in which a wise and intelligent man would do, not with whining and complaining, not with grovelling and cowardice, not with self-pity and resentment, not with bluster and bragga-docio, but with fortitude, patience, and dignity.

Admitting all this, what does it have to do with happiness? For re-member, our entire justification of the good life or the examined life consisted in the fact that this, for a human being, is the happy life. Yet considering the incredibly varied and frightful and unforeseeable misfortunes that can befall a man in the course of his life, is it not being fatuous to say that no matter what may happen to him, all he needs to do in order to be happy is simply to exercise the moral virtues?

It is one thing to recommend the so-called good life on the ground that it is our duty, or what God demands of us, or something of the sort; but it is another thing to recommend it on the ground that only the good life is the happy life. For there is no getting around the fact that human life is fraught with so many perils that even the moral virtue of a Socrates could not guarantee anything that by any stretch of the imagination could be called genuine happiness.

This problem plagued Aristotle himself in the very first book of the *Ethics:*

> Happiness, as we said, requires both complete goodness and a complete lifetime. For many reverses and vicissitudes of all sorts occur in the course of life, and it is possible that the most prosperous man may encounter great disasters in his declining years, as the story is told of Priam in the epics; but no one calls a man happy who meets with misfortunes like Priam's, and comes to a miserable end.[5]

Aristotle's resolution of the problem seems at first reading to be somewhat evasive and disappointing:

> But the accidents of fortune are many and vary in degree of magnitude; and although small pieces of good luck, as also of misfortune, clearly do not change the whole course of life, yet great and repeated successes will render life more blissful, since both of their own nature they help to embellish it, and also they can be nobly and virtuously utilized; while great and frequent reverses can crush and mar our bliss both by the pain they cause and by the hindrance they offer to many activities. Yet nevertheless even in adversity nobility shines through, when a man endures repeated and severe misfortune with patience, not owing to insensibility but from generosity and greatness of soul. And if, as we said, a man's life is determined by his activities, no supremely happy man can ever become miserable. For he will never do hateful or base actions, since we hold that the truly good and wise man will bear all kinds of fortune in a seemly way, and will always act in the noblest manner that the cir-

cumstances allow; even as a good general makes the most effective use of the forces at his disposal, and a good shoemaker makes the finest shoe possible out of the leather supplied him, and so on with all the other crafts and professions. And this being so, the happy man can never become miserable; though it is true he will not be supremely blessed if he encounters the misfortunes of a Priam.[6]

How satisfactory is this as an answer to the challenge that the good life—the life of intellectual and moral virtue—is no guarantee of happiness? Aristotle's concession is a major one: he admits that, in cases of extreme adversity, the good man cannot be said to enjoy full happiness; in fact, he cannot count on much more than the none-too-consoling certainty that he will at least "never become miserable." This, you might say, is a pretty slim recommendation for a life of virtue!

It is well to keep in mind what Aristotle is trying to prove. He is not concerned to demonstrate that virtue is a sure guarantee of happiness. He is only trying to show that a life of virtue, while not an absolute guarantee of happiness, is the best guarantee there is, and that the good man, while he may not be completely happy under circumstances of adversity, is at least happier under such circumstances than the non-virtuous man would be. In other words, the Aristotelian contention is that only by living in a truly human way—i.e., by exercising the intellectual and moral virtues—can a human being assure himself of leading as happy and as full a life as circumstances will permit.

In the light of such considerations it is the part of wisdom to acknowledge that there is another dimension to ethics, over and above the dimension of the purely human and the properly philosophical. In such a dimension one can only have faith that "the Lord is my stony rock, and my defense; my Savior, my God, and my might, in whom I will trust, my buckler, the horn also of my salvation, and my refuge."[7] This, however, is to pass beyond philosophy and enter into the precincts of religion; but to go beyond philosophy is to go beyond the province of this book.

7

But What If God Is Dead?

1. Introduction

"God is dead." This was Nietzsche's proclamation, and nowadays, it is something that nearly everyone accepts without question. The proposition has come to be such a truism that no one remembers to give Nietzsche the credit for it. We don't even bother to proclaim it any more; we just act on it. For the import of Nietzsche's proclamation is simply that there is no objectively grounded moral order anywhere in the universe:* morality can appeal neither to God nor to nature nor to reality of any kind as sources from which it may derive its basis and its justification. And "if the belief in God and in an essentially moral ordering of things is no longer tenable," why not accept the consequence, viz., "the belief in the absolute immorality of nature and in the utter purposelessness and meaninglessness of our psychologically necessary human impulses and affections"?[1]

The purpose of the present book is to suggest that, in Nietzsche's terms, God is not dead after all, that nature itself, or at least human nature, does involve a moral order, which it should be the concern of human beings to recognize and to act upon. Yet we still have not fully

---

*It goes almost without saying that the statement "There is no moral order in the universe" is neither equivalent to, nor a necessary consequence of, the statement "God is dead." However, both Nietzsche and Sartre do consider that in the modern world the loss of faith in a moral order is in fact consequent upon the loss of faith in God. Hence they tend to use the two statements as if they were practically interchangeable. We shall follow this usage in both the present chapter and the next.

and honestly faced up to the fact that Nietzsche's dictum is widely accepted by our contemporaries, and might well be used as the epigraph of practically every contemporary treatise on ethics. In our first chapter we argued that ethical relativism and skepticism are untenable and inconsistent; but we have still to meet head-on the unshakable current conviction that ethics has no objective basis or foundation whatever. To this end, it will be appropriate to consider certain characteristic examples of present-day ethical positions, in which an attempt is made to convert Nietzsche's ethical skepticism into a position of strength.

2. Utilitarianism

A. THE INDIFFERENCE OF UTILITARIANISM TO QUESTIONS REGARDING AN OBJECTIVE BASIS FOR ETHICS

With a combination of naïve exuberance and English smugness, Jeremy Bentham confidently insisted that the whole business of morals and ethics could be reduced simply to a matter of promoting the greatest happiness of the greatest number. This position makes sense to many men and women living in present-day society. Why worry about whether nature is amoral, or whether our psychologically determined feelings and impulses have any meaning? We know what we want, don't we? So let's try to get what we want, and get it for as many of our fellow human beings as we can, without troubling ourselves over whether this principle of conduct is sanctioned by God or by nature or by some ultimate moral order of the universe.

B. ALTRUISM AS AN ETHICAL RED HERRING

Another feature of this utilitarian program recommends it to many people, although it might have disturbed some of the original proponents of the doctrine, particularly John Stuart Mill. Most people today, we would suggest, tend to assume that morals or ethics involves only their relations with others and never their relations with themselves. Everyone knows what he himself likes and enjoys, what would be a source of pleasure and happiness to himself. The problem thus is not one of knowing what one wants, but of knowing how to get it without injuring too many other people and depriving them of what *they* want. From such a standpoint morality consists in nothing but having regard for others. One has no obligation to pursue one's own happiness; one will do that anyhow; but one does have an obligation to consider the happiness of others, the greatest happiness of the greatest number.

The utilitarians have always had some difficulty in showing why anyone has any obligation to think about others. If one begins by basing one's ethics on straightforward hedonistic principles, asserting that pleasure is the only thing of any value in life and recommending that the moral agent simply do as he pleases, it is patently difficult to make the transition from such a starting point to the further assertion that this same moral agent ought to concern himself not merely with his own pleasure, but equally with the pleasure of others.

To be sure, a utilitarian can try to justify having regard for others simply on the ground that this is in one's own best interests. This would be an altruism based on purely egoistic grounds. But, as has often been remarked, this would not be genuine altruism at all: the happiness of others or the greatest happiness of the greatest number would not be intrinsically valuable or worth while; the only value attaching to the happiness of others would be the purely instrumental one that it would somehow contribute to one's own greater happiness.

Again, one can try to launch an argument, involving purely logical or linguistic considerations, to show that it can't be just one's own happiness that is of value, but rather the happiness of all, or at least the greatest happiness of the greatest number. Many people will recall Mill's argument to this effect:

> Questions about ends are, in other words, questions what things are desirable. The utilitarian doctrine is that happiness is desirable, and the only thing desirable, as an end; all other things being only desirable as means to that end. What ought to be required of this doctrine, what conditions is it requisite that the doctrine should fulfill—to make good its claim to be believed?
>
> The only proof capable of being given that an object is visible is that people actually see it. The only proof that a sound is audible is that people hear it; and so of the other sources of our experience. In like manner, I apprehend, the sole evidence it is possible to

produce that anything is desirable is that people do actually desire it. If the end which the utilitarian doctrine proposes to itself were not, in theory and in practice, acknowledged to be an end, nothing could ever convince any person that it was so. No reason can be given why the general happiness is desirable, except that each person, so far as he believes it to be attainable, desires his own happiness. This, however, being a fact, we have not only all the proof which the case admits of, but all which it is possible to require, that happiness is a good, that each person's happiness is a good to that person, and the general happiness, therefore, a good to the aggregate of all persons.[2]

As stated, this argument is dubious, to say the least. Whether it can be saved from collapse by a more subtle formulation of the refutation of egoism in the manner of G. E. Moore[3] is a question with which we need not concern ourselves here. Nevertheless utilitarianism does commend itself to many people, as an ethical doctrine that seems to rest on no more than the fact that human beings know the difference between being happy and being miserable. It commends itself for the very reason that it requires no questionable presupposition of a moral order rooted in the nature of things. It commends itself, also, as a doctrine which tends to center our moral concern almost exclusively on the welfare and happiness of others. For some strange reason most people today seem to assume that morality begins and ends with helping others. Utilitarianism appeals to them because it fits their preconceived notions[4] of what an ethical or moral theory should be.

Whether or not such a utilitarian type of altruism can be justified, any such identification of ethics with altruism is radically at variance with the sort of ethics of the rational man that we have been trying to defend in this book. In Aristotle's eyes ethics does not begin with thinking of others, it begins with oneself. The reason is that every human being faces the task of learning how to live, how to be a human being, just as he has to learn how to walk or to talk. No one can be truly human, can live and act as a rational man, without first going through the difficult and often painful business of acquiring the intellectual and moral virtues, and then, having acquired them, actually exercising them in the concrete, but tricky, business of living.

This is not to say that for Aristotle ethics has no concern with the welfare of others. Nor are we arguing that Aristotle is necessarily any more successful than the utilitarians in providing an adequate justification for the obligation, which is certainly incumbent upon us all, to concern ourselves with the rights and the well-being of our fellow men. Personally, I think that Aristotle does provide a better justification than the utilitarians. But since the investigation in this book is restricted to individual ethics, as contrasted with social ethics, to problems of the individual's development and perfection as contrasted with those of the state and society, we can pass over this issue as not being relevant to our present purpose.

C. THE INSUFFICIENCIES OF TRYING TO CONCEIVE HAPPINESS APART FROM ANY OBJECTIVE CRITERION

To return to questions that are relevant, we observed earlier that in the eyes of many people nowadays there is no problem in defining what they themselves want or what would make them happy or be best for them; the only problem is whether in pursuing their own best interests they may come into conflict with the interests of others. Socrates, however, far from supposing that everyone pretty much knows what is best for him, assumes that the primary, if not the exclusive, problem of ethics is precisely that of knowing oneself. In the light of our whole rather elaborate analysis of the human moral situation, can any of us any longer be under any misapprehension as to what fools we mortals be? We do not know ourselves, we are forever deluding ourselves, making ourselves believe we are something which we are not, trying always to strike a pose or to act a part, refusing constantly to see ourselves as others see us.

The source of this self-blindness, which utilitarianism so often seems to foster, can be located in that very tendency on the part of utilitarian moralists to try to erect an ethics merely on the basis of human pleasure and happiness, and not on the basis of human nature or the moral order of nature as whole. Nothing would seem to be easier than for a man to be contented with himself, when in fact the self he is so contented with falls woefully short of what his self might be expected to be, in the light of man's natural human capacities for an intelligent and examined life. The example of Sir Walter Elliott should be enough to convince us that the whole task of morals and ethics is not to make men happy and contented; on the contrary, the task of ethics is to make them unhappy with what they are at present, to rouse them from their smugness and complacency. For in Aristotle's eyes the thing to be sought in life is not happiness as such, but happiness or satisfaction in the attainment of one's natural human end of perfection. This is why we earlier spoke of Aristotle's "objective definition"[5] of happiness and of his effort to make of happiness something objectively determinable.

To make this point against the utilitarians, we have cited the happy and satisfied existence of Sir Walter Elliott. We might even more aptly have used the example of Marcel's "man on the Underground,"[6] whose life was obviously blighted and miserable when judged by the standards of men's natural human capacities, but who nevertheless might have been thoroughly happy and satisfied with his own estimate of himself.

Now, perhaps, we can begin to see how Huxley's *Brave New World* is a far more devastating refutation of utilitarianism than all the subtle and elaborate philosophical arguments that one can muster. Huxley clearly perceives, as we all must nowadays if we stop to think about it, that the most efficient and painless way of achieving the greatest happiness of the greatest number is to condition human beings so as to make them unquestioningly and unquestionably happy in their roles as Alphas, Betas, Gammas, or Deltas of the twentieth-century Leviathan.

As the Controller reminded the Savage,

"You can't make flivvers without steel—and you can't make tragedies without social instability. The world's stable now. People are happy; they get what they want, and they never want what they can't get. They're well off; they're safe; they're never ill; they're not afraid of death; they're blissfully ignorant of passion and old age; they're plagued with no mothers or fathers; they've got no wives, or children, or lovers to feel strongly about; they're so conditioned that they practically can't help behaving as they ought to behave. And if anything should go wrong, there's *soma*. Which you go and chuck out of the window in the name of liberty, Mr. Savage. *Liberty!*" He laughed. "Expecting Deltas to know what liberty is! And now expecting them to understand *Othello!* My good boy!"

The Savage was silent for a little. "All the same," he insisted obstinately, "*Othello's* good, *Othello's* better than those feelies."

"Of course it is," the Controller agreed. "But that's the price we have to pay for stability. You've got to choose between happiness and what people used to call high art. We've sacrificed the high art. We have the feelies and the scent organ instead."

"But they don't mean anything."

"They mean themselves; they mean a lot of agreeable sensations to the audience."[7]

John Stuart Mill himself recognized this sort of danger when he declared, "It is better to be a human being dissatisfied than a pig satisfied; better to be Socrates dissatisfied than a fool satisfied."[8] But in thus voicing his own honest convictions, Mill utterly betrayed his own utilitarian principles. Besides, Mill lived in the comfortable Victorian era. Had he lived today, when totalitarian dictators seem to possess such limitless resources for making men happy by turning them into pigs and fools, one wonders whether Mill would not have been among the first to recognize that mere pleasure and happiness, when understood in abstraction from the moral requirement of man's nature as a human being, so far from being sufficient criteria of the good life, may well prove to be the instruments of man's utter degradation and brutalization.

3. G. E. Moore and the problem of the naturalistic fallacy

A. PHILOSOPHICAL SOPHISTICATION AND UTILITARIANISM

But isn't all this criticism of utilitarianism rather like whipping a dead horse? Although utilitarian principles may be among the staple presuppositions of the comparatively uncritical ethical thinking of present-day intellectuals, utilitarianism does not seem to be taken too seriously by academic philosophers. Ever since G. E. Moore propounded his famous argument about the "naturalistic fallacy,"[9] both hedonism and utilitarianism have seemed thoroughly discredited.

Or have they? Ironically enough, while the effect of Moore's argument has been to leave utilitarianism completely undone, it seems to have left undone every other type of ethics as well; nor have more recent English writers on ethics come forward with anything much to take the place of utilitarianism. On the contrary, their activity seems to have been diverted from properly ethical concerns to concern with the mere analysis of ethical language. Should you ask these analysts to what sort of ethics they would be inclined personally to commit themselves, they would probably say that a man's personal commitments are in no wise a philosophical matter, and hence no one's business but their own. Should you persevere, assuring them that you realize that philosophy is above anything so personal as convictions and beliefs, and that all you are doing is manifesting a very unphilosophical curiosity as to what their moral convictions may happen to be, it is just possible that they might come out from behind their sophistication long enough to admit that they were utilitarians, though largely as a matter of course and because they hardly know what else to be. Just try scratching the skin of an up-to-the-minute Oxford philosopher, and you may find that he is nothing but a simple utilitarian underneath.

B. THE NATURALISTIC FALLACY: THE ATTEMPT TO TURN THE MERELY NATURAL INTO THE GOOD

However, we cannot avoid facing up to G. E. Moore's argument regarding the naturalistic fallacy. For this argument not only strikes at the root of utilitarianism, it also appears to cut the ground right out from under the Aristotelian ethical position, according to which the good for man is simply man's natural end, that toward which a human being is naturally oriented simply by virtue of being human. Indeed, all of the considerations which we raised in our first chapter about the separation of fact from value, of the "is" from the "ought"—all these might be said to find their ultimate justification in Moore's exposure of the naturalistic fallacy.

For our purpose, a recapitulation of the argument precisely in Moore's terms might not be very illuminating. Instead we shall attempt to give a somewhat simplified version of it, in order to better exhibit its pertinence in the present context.

As we have seen, for Aristotle "the good" is simply "that at which all things aim."[10] More specifically, with respect to human beings, if you want to know what the human good is, Aristotle's counsel is that you try to determine what it is that man aims at, what his natural end is, what that fullness or perfection is toward which a human being naturally tends. This will never do, Moore thinks, because in such an account of what the human good is, Aristotle is offering at least implicitly, if not explicitly, a definition of goodness;[11] and the definition, unfortunately, commits the naturalistic fallacy.

What is this naturalistic fallacy anyway? In answer to such a question Moore would undoubtedly point out, first, that in his definition of goodness Aristotle seems to equate the good of man, or of anything else for that matter, with that toward which the thing in question naturally tends. The good of an acorn is to be a full-grown oak; the good of man is to lead an examined life.

But there is something very dubious, Moore thinks, about this attempt to identify the good of anything with that toward which it naturally tends. Why should a natural tendency necessarily be a tendency toward the good? To confine our attention to human beings for the moment, why should the mere fact that I aim at something, or that you do, or that all men do, necessarily mean that what we are aiming at is good? Is it not at least conceivable that what men do in fact aim at might well be anything but good, might even be evil, or might be neither one nor the other?

In other words, Moore is accusing Aristotle of trying to convert a mere fact of nature into a value, and it can't be done. In order to see that this is what Aristotle is up to, let us briefly recapitulate the main considerations in support of the Aristotelian view that man's natural end is simply to live intelligently. To begin with, Aristotle urges that the characteristic end for a human being cannot be simply to stay alive in the manner of a vegetable. Neither can it be to live on an animal level, since even a cow or a horse does this. Therefore, Aristotle concludes, man's true end can only be to use the intelligence which he alone possesses—to live intelligently, to lead an examined life.

Suppose that, for the purposes of argument, we admit that the examined life is man's natural end. Does that prove that it is good? Moore would say "No." Yet this is precisely what Aristotle must undertake to show if his argument is to have any pertinence for ethics. But he cannot show this, since his argument commits the naturalistic fallacy, being an attempt to pass from the fact that something is natural to the fact that it is good, from the "is" to the "ought,"[12] from fact to value.

C. THE CONCEIVABILITY OF THE OPPOSITE AS THE CRITERION OF THE NATURALISTIC FALLACY

But we still have not gotten to the root of the fallacy as Moore sees it. Moore is not content to rest his case simply on the seeming implausibility of Aristotle's equation of fact with value, of the natural with the good. Moore wants also to show that this is logically impossible, because Aristotle has violated the logical criteria of good definition. How has he done so?

By way of answer, we might note that the epigraph of Moore's book is a quotation from Bishop Butler: "Everything is what it is, and not another thing." Accordingly, to define a thing, one must define it as what it is and not as something else. No one could very well take exception to this. But it is not hard to guess what the thrust of such a truism is likely to be in the present context. Moore is obviously going to insist that to define the good as that at which all things aim—or, more accurately, to define the good of anything as that at which it aims or toward which it tends by nature—clearly violates Butler's canon, for it defines the good as the natural, i.e., it defines it not as what it is, but rather as something else. It equates value with fact, the "ought" with the "is."

What's more, Moore thinks he has a touchstone by which he can determine in any given case, and particularly in the instant case of Aristotle, whether a definition does violate the canon of never equating the thing to be defined with anything other than itself. The device is this: if a definition of a thing is a legitimate definition, it must be such that its opposite is simply inconceivable or self-contradictory. Thus suppose the definition of x to be thus and so, say, "y." Then it must be absolutely inconceivable that x should be other than y. For to suppose otherwise would be like saying that it was conceivable that x might be other than x, which is absurd.

Applying this touchstone to the Aristotelian definition of the good, the latter is at once found to be wanting, Moore thinks. As we have already seen, no sooner does one try to identify the good of a thing with that toward which it is naturally ordered or toward which it naturally tends, than the question immediately becomes meaningful and pertinent: is such a natural end necessarily good, after all; might not the natural in this case be anything but good? In other words, the opposite of the proposed definition is at least conceivable; and if so, then the definition is not a proper definition at all.

Nor does Moore stop with this. Suppose that instead of trying to equate the good with the object of some natural tendency, we tried to equate it with some other natural property, say, with the pleasant as the hedonists propose, or with the desired, or with any object of any interest, as R. B. Perry held. In each of these cases the same touchstone can be applied and with the same result. For instance, one can quite meaningfully ask with respect to the hedonistic definition: "But if a thing is pleasant, does that necessarily mean that it is good?" No more is needed than that such a question should be meaningful, in order to show that the proposed definition is no definition at all.

Apparently, then, according to Moore's criterion goodness cannot be equated with any natural property at all, or with any supernatural property either. It cannot be equated with any other property of any kind whatever. The property of goodness, therefore, cannot be identified with any property save that of goodness itself; which means that it cannot be defined at all. It is an indefinable property, as Moore would say.

D. THE NATURALISTIC FALLACY ENTRAPS ITS OWN INVENTOR

So much for Moore's point about the naturalistic fallacy. The point is certainly ingenious, but is it sound? The interesting thing about it is that it seeks to upset Aristotle's account of goodness—or for that matter any account of goodness, whether naturalistic or supernaturalistic—not by an appeal to the facts, but by an appeal to logic. Aristotle's definition of the good is held to be mistaken, not because it does not fit the facts, but because it violates the logical canons of good definition: it attempts to define something not in terms of what it is, but in terms of what it is not.

Unassailable as this seems, one wonders whether Moore may not have argued himself into a cul-de-sac. If any definition of the good must commit a fallacy, then on the same principles just about any definition of anything must also commit a fallacy. If one defines A as A, this is merely a tautology, not a definition. On the other hand, if one defines A as B or C, then one is defining A in terms of what is other than A, and this violates the principle that everything is what it is and not another thing. However, one must define A either in terms of A or in terms of something other than A. Hence, on such principles, it would seem impossible ever to define anything. And this is far more than Moore himself ever bargained for.[13]

Nor is this all. Moore insists that the criterion of any genuine definition is that its opposite is inconceivable, because self-contradictory. On the basis of this criterion he was able to rule out Aristotle's definition of good, or any similar definition. From this it follows that no definition can ever be of a form other than that of an empty tautology, A is A. For if the opposite of any proper definition is perforce self-contradictory, then such an opposite will be of the form A is non-A. But then, the definition itself can only be of the form, A is A. This means that a definition can never tell us anything, or convey any sort of information whatever. We can only say that cats are cats, or that yellow is yellow. We cannot really say anything about cats or about yellow. In order to perceive the truth of a statement to the effect that cats are cats, I don't even need to know what a cat is. The statement is true in virtue of its form alone, "A is A." It is a mere formal truth or logical truth. But such a definition as the statement, "Cats are cats," does not really give us any information about cats at all.

Here's a howdy-do. Any definition that meets Moore's criterion must be of a form that makes it quite impossible for it to be a definition at all, at least in the sense of telling us what the thing being defined is. In short, to define anything is, on Moore's principle, to fail to define it, and to aim at knowing what anything is, is to commit oneself to the logical impossibility of ever knowing what it is.

To say, therefore, that Moore's famed doctrine of the naturalistic fallacy is self-defeating is an understatement. The simple truth is that it is a logical mess, which we need not try to clean up here. We shall content ourselves with a few suggestions as to where Moore seems to have taken a wrong turning.

E. WHERE MOORE WENT WRONG

Suppose we grant that everything is what it is and not another thing. Does it follow from this that as soon as we think we have found out what a given thing is, it must at once become impossible that we could ever be wrong? According to Moore, if it *is* conceivable that we might be wrong, then this in itself is sufficient indication that we do not know what the thing in question is. This does seem far-fetched. What we are suggesting is that while we may grant Moore his basic principle, taken from Butler, we cannot grant him his criterion for determining whether or not our knowledge of a thing (i.e., our definition of that thing) is accurate knowledge. He held, you remember, that if a definition is legitimate, its opposite must be inconceivable or self-contradictory. Thus it is Moore's criterion of definition, not Butler's principle, that causes all the trouble.

Once we discard Moore's criterion,* and continue our efforts to know things for what they are, it will always be meaningful to ask whether what, in a given instance, we have supposed something to be is really what that thing is. We can ask such a question without prejudicing the possibility that what we have supposed a given thing to be is what it actually is, or that what we have taken the thing's definition to be is really its definition. To take a crude illustration, we may suppose

---

*It will be noted that our repudiation of Moore's criterion rests upon two kinds of consideration. According to the one, the criterion must be repudiated because it leads to a *reductio ad absurdum*. According to the other, the criterion should be repudiated because, at least commonsensically, it is gratuitous: we do in fact constantly question our definition of things as to their soundness and adequacy, without for that reason supposing our proposed definitions not even to be definitions. Nevertheless, this still leaves untouched the strictly logical point which is presumably the ultimate strong point for any defense of Moore's criterion, namely, that a definition being a statement of what a thing is, viz., A is A, its opposite will be simply a contradiction, viz., A is not A. This logical point, however, is one which we cannot attempt to deal with in the present essay.

that there are such things as human beings and that they are what they are and not anything else. We may suppose further that in answer to the question, "What is a human being?" we give as our definition, "A human being is a rational animal." And we may then raise the question whether or not this is the right definition of "human being" without prejudicing the possibility that it *is* the right definition.

More generally, of any natural kind of species—silver, amoebas, hydrogen, electricity—we can ask what such types or kinds of thing are and we can offer definitions of them. Then we can always ask ourselves: "Is my definition correct? Is the kind of thing I am considering really of the sort I have supposed it to be? Or must I change my definition?" Because questions of this kind are always meaningful, it does not follow that the things we encounter in the world are undefinable, or that any attempted definition of them must be either unquestionable or else not a definition at all. That would be fantastic.

Indeed, if we mistake not, what Moore's criterion of definition amounts to is something like this: if a rational animal is simply what a human being is, if this is what we mean by "man," then it should be as absurd to ask whether man is, after all, really a rational animal, as it is to ask whether man is man or not. To use such a criterion of definition seems both gratuitous and far-fetched.

To return, then, to Aristotle and his proposed definition of the good as that at which all things aim, why shouldn't it be perfectly proper to ask whether such a definition is sound or adequate? Is this really what we mean by "good"? Is that at which something naturally aims necessarily good? But if Moore is right, and if what Aristotle is proposing as a definition of "good" is properly a definition, then it is as absurd to ask whether the good is really that at which all things aim as it would be to ask whether the good is the good.

Isn't it obvious that Moore's criterion of definition is too severe? As regards Aristotle and his proposed definition of "good," isn't the real question whether his definition is sound, not whether his definition is a definition? Aristotle may have been entirely mistaken in his conception of the nature of goodness. Yet merely because it is conceivable that he may have been mistaken, we cannot say for that reason alone that his definition is not even a definition because it commits the naturalistic fallacy. It may not be a good definition, but surely it isn't logically or linguistically fallacious. But if not, then isn't this whole business about the naturalistic fallacy nothing more than a red herring?

Having thus (we hope) cleared the naturalistic fallacy out of our path, we can now go ahead and try to understand goodness and value in terms of real tendencies and dispositions in nature. We may even hope that if the bugbear of Moore's naturalistic fallacy can be removed, there is a chance that British moral philosophers may once more take heart and actually seek to find real distinctions between good and bad, and right and wrong.

F. THE NATURALISTIC FALLACY AS A SOURCE OF SKEPTICISM

It was certainly not Moore's intention that his doctrines should influence ethical thinkers in a skeptical direction; but this is precisely the effect that they have, by and large, tended to produce. Moore seemed to feel that he had only to show that notions of value could not possibly be understood in terms of the facts of nature, and philosophers would immediately recognize that value terms would have to designate properties that were somehow non-natural. But subsequent thinkers concluded otherwise. They contended that the argument designed to show that value terms could not designate natural properties also showed that such terms did not designate properties at all. Hence words like "good" and "bad," "right" and "wrong," were not descriptive of anything in the real world; in fact, they just weren't descriptive. In the final analysis there could be no sense in seeking to know what the good life is or whether a certain action is right or wrong, for these things cannot be matters of knowledge, since it is a simple fact of logic—and indirectly a fact of life too—that moral and ethical judgments are ultimately non-cognitive.

Contemporary English writers on ethics are quite as convinced as Nietzsche that God is dead. But being committed to the British practice of understatement, they would never dream of uttering dramatic, Zarathustra-like pronouncements on the subject. They would only treat defenders of God or of a moral order with supercilious contempt, much as they would treat a man who ate peas with his knife. To anyone so naïve as to speak of a divinely grounded or naturally grounded moral order they would merely say, "My good man, don't you realize that you are committing the naturalistic fallacy?"

G. THE OLD BUGBEAR OF THE SEPARATION OF FACT AND VALUE; LET'S HAVE DONE WITH IT

Granting that a deliverance from the naturalistic fallacy is also a deliverance from the mortmain of contemporary English ethics, we are still far from having established that the good is that at which all things aim. All we have done so far has been to show that such a definition of "good" is not logically or linguistically fallacious. But this still does not prove that the definition is correct.

In fact, must we not admit that in the Aristotelian definition, the good is being defined in terms of a natural property, that value is being equated with fact? If so, then is not Aristotle defining goodness and value, not in terms of what they are, but in terms of something which they definitely are not?

Evidently we can no longer evade facing up to the problem of the separation of fact and value. If these are separate and incommensurable, as is customarily assumed, then there is no way in which, through a consideration of the natural order of things, we can ever determine the moral order of things. If fact and value are wholly separate and distinct, then no investigation of the facts of human nature can ever disclose what human good is or what is the good life for man. As we remarked in the preceding section, it makes not the slightest difference how convincingly it can be shown that the examined life is the life toward which man is ordered and directed by nature. That still will not prove that the examined life is the good life, unless it can first be shown that, with respect to any being, not only human beings, that toward which such a being is naturally ordered is the good of that being. From such a proposition it would certainly follow that man's natural end is man's true good. But without such a major premise, the latter conclusion must appear baseless and without warrant.

What, then, of this major premise? What of Aristotle's own formulation of the principle, "The good is that at which *all* things aim"? How may this be substantiated? The answer we must give to such questions may seem not only unduly simple, but unduly dogmatic. For we propose to challenge directly the initial separation of values from facts, and we should like to suggest, instead, that all facts, if not identical with values, at least have value aspects.

The opposite view may have arisen from an excessively static and atomistic conception of facts; if we put this conception out of our minds, the whole picture changes. Look at it this way: is there any fact at all that does not suggest all sorts of possibilities of how it might become other and different? Is there any fact at all that has not proceeded from some prior state of facts, this last having been, as it were, big with the new fact even before the latter came into being? In other words, the whole of reality is shot through with the distinction between potentiality and actuality, between what is still only able to be and what actually is. The potential is related to the actual as the imperfect to the perfect, the incomplete to the complete, the empty to the full.

And what about goodness? Why not consider that, in this all-embracing context, the good is simply the actual as related to the potential? It is that toward which the potential is ordered and directed, that which fulfills and completes and actualizes it. The good, in other words, is any actual state or condition of things which is the fulfillment or completion of some prior state that was only potential with respect to it.

On such a view there is clearly a sense in which "good" is not an absolute term at all, for anything that is good is always good for, or of, or with reference to, something else. One might even tear a leaf from some of the contemporary English writers and say that "good" does not designate a "property" of things at all—"property" being a quality like redness or weight. But one cannot conclude from this that "good" is therefore not a descriptive term. Rather it is a term which always points to that relational posture of things according to which anything that exists can always be compared both to what it might be but as yet is not, and to what formerly might have been it, or could have become it, but which now is no more, having actually become it.

"But," you will say, "this can hardly be a true account of things, for in the natural sciences we do not consider the facts of nature as being thus intimately associated with values and as each having its own value aspects or value relationships." To which the answer is that if science chooses to abstract from, or not to consider, the value aspects of things or the value-relatedness of things, that is science's privilege; but this does not mean that things in the natural world are not shot through with relations of potencies to acts and of acts to potencies, with the result that nothing in the natural world, no fact of nature, is ever really separated from its own value aspects. Values are always there in nature, if we choose to look for them.

Thus to anyone who feels it simply incredible that facts should ever imply values or that "is" should ever imply "ought," our reply is that it is far more incredible that these two should ever have been separated in the first place. Moreover, if we mistake not, the reason such a separation has come to be generally accepted nowadays, and even to seem almost self-evident, is that the attempt to associate the two is always made to appear as an exception and an anomaly. Accustomed as we are to identifying the natural world with the scientific universe, and values having been excluded from the scientific universe altogether and *a priori,* it is not surprising that we should take it as a matter of course that water flows downhill not because it ought to, but simply because it does, or that an acorn develops into an oak, not because this is best for the acorn, but simply because this is the way acorns are in fact observed to behave. Accordingly, when against this background we turn to consider our human values and the judgments of success or failure that in our everyday lives we pass upon ourselves and others, it is bound to seem as though such judgments were concerned with something outside the realm of nature.

But is this anything more than a simple distortion or loss of perspective? For no sooner do we go behind the somewhat artificial construct of the scientific universe, and consider the lived world of every day, where things are everywhere in process of change and development, where one kind of thing naturally changes or matures in its accustomed way and another thing in its different way, where certain things have their capacities and potentialities and others theirs—when once we place ourselves in this lived context of our everyday lives, then ends and goals, values and purposes, healthy specimens and diseased ones, the perfect and the imperfect, the good and the bad, all of these come to be recognized as things that are natural, not exceptional or anomalous. We do not have to apologize and try to make room for the ideas of change and of value, or consider them as concepts valid only with reference to our human purposes. On the contrary, the whole of nature is permeated with values; we cannot conceive the natural world as stripped of values, unless we conceive of it as stripped of all those manifold and varied powers, capacities, potentialities, and abilities which characterize the objects of nature. The good of any thing is to that thing as the actual is to the potential.

At the same time, it should be noted that since values and "goods" are always values and "goods" *for* something, it is understandable that as human beings we should be almost exclusively concerned with what is valuable and good for ourselves and for man. For this reason—to revert to our old example—while the full-grown oak may be the acorn's good, that is, its natural end, it is not, clearly, the natural end of man. We might choose to call a tree "good" because it happened to serve our human purposes. But that it should be something good or of value for the undeveloped seed does not usually occur to us; nor should we be inclined in such a context to ascribe to it such terms as "good" or "valuable." But it would nonetheless *be* good, if the good is defined simply as the perfect with respect to the imperfect, the complete with respect to the incomplete, the actual with respect to the potential.

And what about this way of defining "good"? Is it the correct definition after all? We should not make any claims to absolute certainty on this score, certainty being no doubt unattainable by finite, fallible human beings. Moreover, as we have made clear in our opposition to Moore, this definition of "good" is not one the opposite of which is inconceivable or self-contradictory. But it is a plausible definition, and many signs point to its soundness. Also it is based on the assumption that, though fact and value are by no means the same thing, they are nevertheless inseparable, in certain respects at least. If they are inseparable, it is a meaningful enterprise to try to discover the good for man by investigating the nature of man—or for that matter, the good of anything by investigating its nature.

8

Existentialism and the Claims
of Irrational Man

1. Existentialism as presupposing the death of God

Many may still wonder how the foregoing rather academic defense
of the Aristotelian principle of the good can serve as a means of raising
God from the dead, in Nietzsche's phrase. Nietzsche's rather flamboy-
ant language might lead one to think that in the modern age something more has died than merely the objectivity of value.

We have been primarily concerned with showing how morals and
ethics can, after all, be based on the facts of nature and on a due regard for the nature of things, particularly the nature of man. Now we
must turn our attention to a challenge to this contention which ema-
nates not from contemporary English thinkers, but from thinkers who,
curiously enough, seem to be utter strangers to the English—their colleagues on the Continent. For want of a better term, we shall refer to
them all loosely as "existentialists," however imprecise this term may
be in any given case. Our discussion of "existentialism" will be neither
complete nor exhaustive. We shall arbitrarily select certain current existentialist themes in order to bring out the contrast, and also certain
points of comparison, between an Aristotelian ethics of rational man
and an existentialist ethics of irrational man.

The ethics of rational man involves as its basic imperative the simple
injunction to be rational, to live intelligently, to exercise the intellectual and moral virtues. The absolute presupposition of this ethics of
rationality and the examined life is the possibility that a human being
can actually come to know what the good life is and what it is incumbent upon him as a human being to do. But such knowledge is possible

only if there are certain objective values in nature—if God, in fact, is not dead but alive.

From the existentialist point of view, as we are rather arbitrarily construing it, there is no value or good in things whatever. Existence is essentially ugly, meaningless, and absurd. Mr. Barrett has skillfully brought this out by an apt contrast between the medieval religious attitude and the current existentialist attitude:

> The waning of religion is a much more concrete and complex fact than a mere change in conscious outlook; it penetrates the deepest strata of man's total psychic life. . . . The loss of the Church was the loss of a whole system of symbols, images, dogmas, and rites which had the psychological validity of immediate experience, and within which hitherto the whole psychic life of Western man had been safely contained. In losing religion, man lost the concrete connection with a transcendent realm of being; he was set free to deal with this world in all its brute objectivity. But he was bound to feel homeless in such a world, which no longer answered the needs of his spirit. A home is the accepted framework which habitually contains our life. To lose one's psychic container is to be cast adrift, to become a wanderer upon the face of the earth. Henceforth, in seeking his own human completeness man would have to do for himself what he once had done for him, unconsciously, by the Church, through the medium of its sacramental life.[1]

Again, in connection with a discussion of Faulkner, Barrett remarks:

> The brute, irrational, given quality of the world comes through so strongly in Faulkner's peculiar technique that he actually shows, and does not merely state, the meaning of the quotation from which his title is derived:
> "[Life] is a tale,
> Told by an idiot, full of sound and fury,
> Signifying nothing."
> Shakespeare places these lines in the context of a fairly well-made tragedy in which evil is destroyed and good triumphs; but Faulkner shows us the world of which Shakespeare's statement would be true;

a world opaque, dense, and irrational, that could not have existed for Shakespeare, close as he was still to medieval Christianity.[2]

The issue need not be posed, as Barrett poses it, in religious terms. It can be understood as a purely philosophical or ethical one: on the one side, there is what we have chosen to call the ethics of rational man; on the other, an ethics in which there can be no meaning whatever to the injunction that a man be rational. Why, on the latter alternative, is such an injunction meaningless? Not because man is not a rational animal, but because reason cannot tell man anything about how to live or what to live for. Human intelligence is powerless and useless in an ethical context because no ethical truth can be found anywhere in the universe. Study nature as you will and you will find nothing of an ethical or moral import: there is no objective moral order; hence existence is meaningless and absurd.

Nevertheless, among the existentialists the supposed death of God has not led to a complete skepticism in regard to ethics, as it seems to have done among contemporary British thinkers; instead, on the Continent the consequence seems to have been the emergence of a new and different ethics, an ethics of irrational man. As Sartre puts it very movingly:

The existentialist, on the contrary, finds it extremely embarrassing that God does not exist, for there disappears with Him all possibility of finding values in an intelligible heaven. There can no longer be any good *a priori,* since there is no infinite and perfect consciousness to think it. It is nowhere written that "the good" exists, that one must be honest or must not lie, since we are now upon the plane where there are only men. Dostoevsky once wrote "If God did not exist, everything would be permitted"; and that, for existentialism, is the starting point. Everything is indeed permitted if God does not exist, and man is in consequence forlorn, for he cannot find anything to depend upon either within or outside himself. He discovers forthwith, that he is without excuse. For if indeed existence precedes essence, one will never be able to explain one's action by reference to a given and specific human nature; in other words, there is no determinism — man is free, man is freedom. Nor, on the other hand, if God does not exist, are we provided with any values or commands that could legitimize our behavior. Thus we have neither behind us, nor before us in a luminous realm of values, any means of justification or excuse. We are left alone, without excuse. That is what I mean when I say that man is condemned to be free. Condemned, because he did not create himself, yet is nevertheless at liberty, and from the moment that he is thrown into this world he is responsible for everything he does. The existentialist does not believe in the power of passion. He will never regard a grand passion as a destructive torrent upon which a man is swept into certain actions as by fate, and which, therefore, is an excuse for them. He thinks that man is responsible for his passion. Neither will an existentialist think that a man can find help through some sign being vouchsafed upon earth for his orientation: for he thinks that the man himself interprets the sign as he chooses. He thinks that every man, without any support or help whatever, is condemned at every instant to invent man. As Ponge has written in a very fine article, "Man is the future of man." . . . If [this] means that, whatever man may now appear to be, there is a future to be fashioned, a virgin future that awaits him—then it is a true saying. But in the present one is forsaken.[3]

On the fundamental issue of whether or not God does exist, whether there is an objective basis for ethics in the nature of things— on this issue we have perhaps already had enough to say. Rather than broach this question again, it might be more interesting to consider certain other aspects of the existentialist critique of the ethics of rational man. For there is a sense in which one might almost say that for the existentialist, even if God or an objective moral order did exist, still, if a human being were to act on such knowledge, the result would be a human personality that would be, in existentialist eyes, far from admirable and far from authentic.

2. *The supposed antithesis between rationality and commitment*

In the passage quoted above Sartre hinted at an interesting point. Having shown how a human being longs for a real moral order which he can "depend upon," whether it be "within or without himself," how he wishes for "some sign to be vouchsafed upon earth for his orientation," Sartre then goes on to remark that even if there were such a sign, it would be "man himself who would be obliged to interpret the sign as he chooses."

At least part of what Sartre means by this is that even if there were an objective moral order, it would still be up to the individual human being to choose it, to take it upon himself, to commit himself to it. Indeed, without such an act of choice or of will, obedience to moral law would be no more meritorious than obedience to the law of gravity. In both cases he might know what the law is, but his observance of it would not be a matter of choice, and hence certainly not a matter of merit. But if human worth and merit arise, not from knowing what we need to do, but from choosing to do it, then what counts morally and ethically is not so much rational intelligence as responsibility and freedom, in Sartre's sense.

As a criticism of an Aristotelian type of ethics, this involves a rather serious oversimplification. As we have insisted in our earlier chapters, the Aristotelian goal for man is not so much to have knowledge as to choose in accordance with such knowledge—not intelligence, but intelligent action. The moral virtues involved in choice are at least as important as the intellectual virtues, if not more so. The ethics of the rational man is an ethics of the man who chooses freely, though he has the responsibility of choosing intelligently. Hence the ethical position that we have been defending seems to have much in common with certain existentialist themes.

A similar misunderstanding often leads existentialist thinkers to distinguish their ethics from what they take to be the ethics of rational man. No sooner does one emphasize the importance of reason and intelligence in human life and the existence of some sort of objective order or values than one is likely to be accused of sacrificing what Kierkegaard would call subjectivity for objectivity.

The objective tendency, which proposes to make everyone an observer, and in its maximum to transform him into so objective an observer that he becomes almost a ghost, scarcely to be distinguished from the tremendous spirit of the historical past—this tendency naturally refuses to know or listen to anything except what stands in relation to itself. If one is so fortunate as to be of service within the given presupposition, by contributing one or another item of information concerning a tribe perhaps hitherto unknown, which is to be provided with a flag and given a place in the paragraph parade; if one is competent within the given presupposition to assign China a place different from the one it has hitherto occupied in the systematic procession, — in that case one is made welcome. But everything else is divinity-school prattle. For it is regarded as a settled thing, that the objective tendency in direction of intellectual contemplation, is, in the newer linguistic usage, the "ethical" answer to the question of what I "ethically" have to do. . . . The question I would ask is this: *What conclusion would inevitably force itself upon Ethics, if the becoming a subject were not the highest task confronting a human being?*[4] . . .

The only reality to which an existing individual may have a relation that is more than cognitive, is his own reality, the fact that he exists; this reality constitutes his absolute interest. Abstract thought requires him to become disinterested in order to acquire knowledge; the ethical demand is that he become infinitely interested in existing.

The only reality that exists for an existing individual is his own ethical reality. To every other reality he stands in a cognitive relation.[5] . . .

To assert the supremacy of thought is Gnosticism; to make the ethical reality of the subject the only reality might seem to be acosmism. The circumstance that it will seem so to a busy thinker who explains everything, a nimble mind that quickly surveys the entire universe, merely proves that such a thinker has a very humble notion of what the ethical means to the subject. If Ethics were to take away the entire world from such a thinker, letting him keep his own self, he would probably regard such a trifle as not worth keeping, and would let it go with the rest—and so it becomes acosmism. But why does he think so slightingly of his own self? If it were our meaning that he should give up the whole world in order to content himself with another person's ethical reality, he would be justified in regarding the exchange as a dead loss. But his own ethical reality, on the other hand, ought to mean more to him than "heaven and earth and all that therein is," more than the six thousand years of human history, more than both astrology and the veterinary sciences or whatever it is that the age demands, all of which is aesthetically and intellectually a huge vulgarity.[6]

Consider for a minute these specimens of Kierkegaardian eloquence and satire: is there any radical incompatibility between what Kierkegaard is here preaching and Aristotle's ethical teaching, as we have interpreted it? In our very first chapter we were quite as concerned as Kierkegaard with depreciating and even poking fun at contemporary academic knowledge, which always seems to do so little for the knower himself. We set our sights upon a higher kind of knowledge that could be likened to Socrates' "Know thyself": a knowledge that could show us "the way," a "saving" knowledge for the human subject himself.

3. But why not a rational commitment?

There seems to be no incompatibility between knowledge of this sort and what Kierkegaard calls "an infinite interest in existing," "an absolute interest in one's own ethical reality." We would go even further and say that the very man who, to borrow Sartre's words, is intent to "find values in an intelligible heaven," who is determined to find something "to depend upon, either within or outside himself," whose concern is to find "values or commands that could legitimize our behavior"—such a one, we suggest, is perfectly capable of being aware that "the becoming a subject" is "the highest task confronting a human being."

Perhaps Kierkegaard himself would not wholly disagree. Remember that in a passage quoted earlier, speaking of Socrates and Socratic knowledge, he said: "This type of knowledge bears a relation to the existing subject who is infinitely interested in existing."[7]

Suppose now that we stand this statement on end, and assert that *only* through knowledge of an objective moral order of values can "an existing subject" properly fulfill the task of "becoming a subject" or go about satisfying his "infinite interest in existing." With this Kierkegaard would most certainly disagree, and so would any existentialist.

Here is the real issue between existentialism and Aristotelian ethics. The issue is not, as existentialists often pretend, between disinterested, impersonal objectivity on the one hand and a committed subjectivity on the other. Nor is it an issue between knowing and doing, or between a mere detached understanding and an actual choosing. The issue is whether one can ever choose rightly without knowledge—whether there can ever be a properly human commitment to what is not justified in the light of knowledge and understanding. For as we found Aristotle insisting in the first book of the *Ethics,* a distinctively and truly human life can only be an intelligent life.

But this means that the Aristotelian type of the rational man is none other than what some existentialists would depreciatively call "the serious man." As one recent writer on Sartre has put it, what Sartre calls "the spirit of seriousness"

> consists in pretending that moral values do not depend on a human choice but that they are dictated by a "natural law," by hazard, or by divine commands. Something would be morally good or bad as it were white or black. The man who takes refuge in the spirit of seriousness tries to hide from himself that it is human freedom which decides on moral values. He tries to ignore that if man is not the creator of being, he is at least the inventor of moral values. The man who takes refuge in the spirit of seriousness tries to evade moral responsibility.[8]

Even better is Kierkegaard's own account of "the serious man":

> The serious man continues: If he were able to obtain certainty with respect to such a good, so as to know that it is really there, he would venture everything for its sake. The serious man speaks like a wag; it is clear enough that he wishes to make fools of us, like the raw recruit who takes a run in preparation for jumping into the water, and actually takes the run,—but gives the leap a go-by. When the certainty is there he will venture all. But what then does it mean to venture? A venture is the precise correlative of an uncertainty; when the certainty is there the venture becomes impossible. If our serious man acquires the definite certainty that he seeks, he will be unable to venture all; for even if he gives up everything, he

will under such circumstances venture nothing—and if he does not get certainty, our serious man says in all earnest that he refuses to risk anything, since that would be madness. In this way the venture of our serious man becomes merely a false alarm. If what I hope to gain by venturing is itself certain, I do not risk or venture, but make an exchange. Thus in giving an apple for a pear, I run no risk if I hold the pear in my hand while making the exchange.[9]

In the light of such passages, we can offer a rather bald formulation of the contrast between an Aristotelian ethics of rational man and an existentialist ethics of irrational man:

> Aristotle: to be human (i.e., to become subjective) is to act and to choose, but always in the light of knowledge and understanding.
>
> The existentialists: to become subjective (i.e., to be truly human) is to act and to choose, but in the absence of knowledge and under-standing.

On the latter view the gravamen of ethics falls not on the intelligence, but on what in the older terminology would have been called the will. Since existentialists assume that God is dead, the authentic exercise of will must be in the very face of this fact, in the consciousness that there is no God,* no objective order of values, no ground or basis of ethics in the older sense at all. Indeed, to make choices and decisions as if there were a God and as if one's choices could therefore be intelligent and rational—this could only be evidence of bad faith, because there is no God and accordingly there can be no such thing as a rational man or an examined life.

What may be said to all this? Perhaps the less said the better. Yet we do want to say at least one thing more. We propose to recall a point

---

*At this point it should be only too obvious that our earlier adoption of the slogan "God is dead," as being the badge of existentialism, would appear quite unjustified in the case of Kierkegaard. For Kierkegaard is not just a religious, but a Christian, existentialist. Nevertheless, the slogan may be seen to be appropriate even with respect to Kierkegaard, as soon as one recalls that in the slogan the death of God is interpreted as being equivalent to the denial of any sort of objective moral order in nature. And Kierkegaard would have been the first to second the denial of any such order, however much he might have disliked labeling it "the death of God."

made in our earlier refutation of relativism, in order to show that perhaps the existentialists fall into a like inconsistency.

To become a "subject" in Kierkegaard's sense, or to be free in Sartre's sense, must one not face up to the realities of the human situation; must one not put aside all temptation to bad faith and resolutely acknowledge the fact that God is dead? Yet this must surely involve a certain understanding, a knowledge of what the score is. The knowledge and understanding involved will be a morally relevant knowledge, a knowledge that indicates what we should do and what our responsibilities are in the light of the facts. Such knowledge will disclose to us what our true human values are, even if there is no moral order in nature. In short, must not the very dialectic of their own position catch the existentialists up into the logic of "Know thyself" and of the examined life, and ultimately into the ethics of rational man?

4. Conclusion: on "doing what comes naturally"

Still, it is not by any such dialectical arguments that the existentialists are going to be answered effectively. Supposing that the hidden logic of their position does commit them to a sort of inverted and covert theory of human nature, that will scarcely suffice to reinstate at one stroke the entire traditional ethics of rational man. The trouble is that the very notion of human nature, and of nature generally, has apparently turned sour for most modern ethical thinkers, not just for the existentialists, but for the utilitarians, for the relativists, for those bewitched by the naturalistic fallacy, for just about everyone, in fact. For this reason, no one thinks any more of turning to nature and of trying to discover in nature such ways of life as are demanded by our nature as men.

But what if the good man is simply the man who has sense enough to be natural, who has succeeded in achieving a knowledge of himself, as Socrates would put it, and who is willing just to be himself? Such a man would not be afflicted with the current disease of feeling that he must always be striking a pose or acting a part. He would not be haunted by any conviction of his own nothingness, furiously driving himself to be forever creating himself anew, or going beyond himself or authenticating himself in the manner of some fancied Nietzschean *Übermensch*. Nor must it be supposed that the only alternative to this kind of desperate freedom, springing from the fiction of one's own nothingness, is the life of complacency, lethargy, and conformity. This would be to turn the injunction to be yourself into a perverted counsel to forget yourself and to escape from yourself by getting lost in the crowd or by seeking the protective coloration of mere conformity. Rather than anything of this sort, the natural life for a human being can be none other than the examined life, the life in which one comes to know oneself as a human being and, in and through such knowledge, comes to be oneself.

All the same, such words as these will doubtless seem only baffling to the so-called educated man of today. "How can all this talk of the examined life deck itself out in appeals to nature and to the natural?" he will say. "By what possible stretch of the imagination can one pretend that the life of a Socrates is any more natural than that of a Nightingale, and what possible meaning can be given to the recommendation that we turn to nature to find out what the good life and the natural life for us is?"

Once again, protests of this sort spring from that most ingrained of modern prejudices, that of identifying nature with the scientific universe, and the investigation of nature with the procedures of modern science. To rebut such a prejudice, one can only reiterate that while in their capacity as scientists men can attain a knowledge of nature that is literally limitless in its own dimension, yet in respect to other dimensions such a scientific knowledge of nature is both narrowly defined and rigorously restricted, not merely in fact, but in principle. Is it not obvious that men merely as human beings can, by exercising their intelligence, achieve a kind of commonsense understanding of their own nature and of the nature of the world they live in which is different from scientific knowledge, and for which scientific knowledge is no substitute?

Let's take an illustration. Some eight years ago there appeared in a popular college textbook series a short paper by a contemporary psychologist entitled *The Natural Man*.[10] When the reader turns back the cover and looks to see just who or what the natural man is, from the standpoint of scientific psychology, one discovers that the author is hard put to it to find any examples of so seemingly rare a creature. But finally after some hemming and hawing and with no little apology for the fact that the examples are far from perfect, the author suggests that the best examples of natural men are so-called feral men—the wild boy of Aveyron, or the Nuremburg boy, or the wolf-children of India.

Now to the poor moral philosopher who is trying to hold up the natural life of man as being the model of the good life, such a scientific version of the natural may well come as a rude shock. But on further consideration we can see that the psychologist-author is simply excluding from his concept of man's nature all those traits and qualities which human beings come to have as a result of social or cultural influences. Similarly he is excluding anything that human beings may have come to be as a result of the exercise of their intelligence and in virtue of their own plans and purposes and designs. Such things are thought to represent artificial[11] accretions to the native and natural endowments of men, and hence must be abstracted from or thought away, if one is ever to come to understand the natural in man as such.

Undoubtedly such a way of conceiving what is natural to man is not only meaningful, but altogether appropriate to the special scientific concerns of the author. And yet from another point of view is it not equally obvious that the mode of existence of the wolf-children of India is not what we would ordinarily call the natural way of life for a human being, any more than we would consider idiocy or paralysis or insanity to be the natural condition of man? On the contrary, man being a rational or intelligent animal by nature, it may be presumed that the natural life for a human being will be some sort of rational or intelligent life, just as man being by nature a political animal,[12] it may be presumed that the natural life for him will be life in some sort of political and cultural milieu. And just as we would certainly recognize that the way of life of the wild boy of Aveyron was unmistakably an unnatural and even bestial existence for a human being, so also, by extension and *mutatis mutandis,* we would surely say that the life of a Nightingale or a Shaftesbury or a Sir Walter Elliott was a foolish, or miserable, or wasted human existence. Moreover, the standard of our judgment in these latter cases is not unlike our standard in the former: it is a regard for the potentialities of man's nature as man that leads us to say of a Nightingale no less than of a feral man that he somehow falls short of his natural human capacities, that he fails to be fully and truly human.

Seen in this light, "doing what comes naturally" must needs take on a very different meaning. Rather than an Annie with her gun being the obvious tutor for us in such matters, it might better be a Plato or an Aristotle. And rather than that characters like Uncle Jed and Grandpa Bill should serve as exemplars in the business of doing what comes naturally, why not look to a Socrates?

November 17, 2003

Meeting Notice

Dear Central Committee Representative:

The last meeting of the year will be held on November 25, 2003, at 7:00 P.M. The meeting will be held in the basement of the County Administration Building.

Feel free to join us for an OSU-Michigan party on Saturday, November 22nd. "Tailgating" begins at 11:00 A.M. at the Party HQ. Cost if $15 per person / $25 couple. Proceeds will go towards a printer / internet access. We will supply chili, hot dogs, chips and beverages. Hope you can make it.

THERE WILL BE NO MEETING IN DECEMBER!

Democratically yours,

Mike King, Chair
(h) 344-6033

Licking County Democratic Party
Mike King, Chair
1188 Berwyn Lane
Newark, Ohio 43055

COLUMBUS, OH 430 7A
PM
16 NOV
2003

ANTHONY J LISSKA
285 BURTRIDGE RD SW
GRANVILLE OH 43023

1101B

Notes

1. IN QUEST OF ETHICAL KNOWLEDGE

1. *Kierkegaard's Concluding Unscientific Postscript,* trans. by David F. Swenson and Walter Lowrie, Princeton, N.J.: Princeton University Press, 1944, p. 268.

2. C. P. Snow, *The Search,* New York: Charles Scribner's Sons, 1958, pp. 280–82.

3. *The Dialogues of Plato,* trans. by Benjamin Jowett, Oxford: Oxford University Press, 3rd ed., 1892, Vol. II, *Apology,* 29 D–E, 38 A.

4. See above, p. 5.

5. Gabriel Marcel, *The Philosophy of Existence,* New York: Philosophical Library, 1949, pp. 1–3.

6. Aldous Huxley, *Brave New World,* New York: Harper and Brothers, 1946, Foreword, pp. xv–xvi.

7. Ruth Benedict, *Patterns of Culture,* New York: Mentor Books, 1958, p. 206.

8. *Ibid.,* p. 33.

9. *Ibid.,* p. 251.

10. *Ibid.,* p. 257.

11. Benito Mussolini, *Diuturna,* pp. 374–77. Quoted from Helmut Kuhn, *Freedom Forgotten and Remembered,* Chapel Hill, N.C.: University of North Carolina Press, 1943, pp. 17–18.

2. THE EXAMINED LIFE: BACK TO SOCRATES AND ARISTOTLE

1. Aristotle, *The Nicomachean Ethics,* Loeb Library translation, Book I, Ch. 1, 1094a 1–3, 6–10.

2. *Ibid.,* Book I, Ch. 2, 1094a 19–21, 22–27.

3. *Ibid.,* Book I, Ch. 7, 1097a 15–24.

4. *Ibid.,* 1097b 24–1098a 4, slightly altered from Loeb Library version.

5. *Kierkegaard's Concluding Unscientific Postscript,* trans. by David F. Swenson and Walter Lowrie, Princeton, N.J.: Princeton University Press, 1944, p. 281.

6. See above, p. 30.

7. *Nicomachean Ethics,* Book X, Ch. 7, 1177a 18–22.

8. *Ibid.,* 1177b 26–1178a 1.

9. *Ibid.,* 1178a 9–10. Cf. the whole of Ch. 8 and especially 1178b 7–24.

10. G. Lowes Dickinson, *The Greek View of Life,* 12th ed., New York: Doubleday, Page and Co., 1919, p. 142.

11. See above, pp. 6–7.

12. Maurice Merleau-Ponty, *Phénoménologie de la perception,* Foreword, trans. by Alice Koller (mimeo., no date, no publisher), pp. 2, 3, 4.

3. WHY NOT REGARD MORALS AND ETHICS AS SIMPLY AN ART OF LIVING?

1. See above, p. 43.

2. John Dryden, *Absalom and Achitophel. The Poetical Works of John Dryden,* Boston: Houghton Mifflin Co., 1909, pp. 111–12.

3. C. P. Snow, *The Masters,* Garden City, N.Y.: Anchor Books, 1959, pp. 44–45.

4. C. V. Wedgwood, *The King's Peace,* New York: Macmillan Co., 1955, p. 70.

5. *Ibid.,* p. 72.

6. *Ibid.,* pp. 61–62.

7. This is the basic scheme used by St. Thomas Aquinas. For a brief but excellent modern account of this way of classifying the passions, cf. John Wild, *Introduction to Realistic Philosophy,* New York: Harper and Brothers, 1948, Ch. 5, especially pp. 110–12.

8. Cf. P. H. Nowell-Smith, *Ethics,* London: Pelican Books, 1954, pp. 112–21.

9. For a most illuminating treatment of this, cf. Wild, *Introduction to Realistic Philosophy,* pp. 136–44.

10. Jane Austen, *Persuasion,* New York: Oxford University Press, 1930, Ch. 1, p. 1.

11. Erich Fromm, *Man for Himself,* London: Routledge and Kegan Paul, 1949, pp. 68–71.

4. WHY MORALS AND ETHICS ARE NOT SIMPLY AN ART OF LIVING

1. Aristotle, *Nicomachean Ethics,* Book VI, Ch. 5, 1140b 23–25. The translation here used is that of J. A. K. Thomson, *The Ethics of Aristotle,* London: George Allen and Unwin, 1953, p. 156. The bracketed words are my interpolation.

2. *Cf. ibid.,* Book II, ch. 6.

3. See above, Ch. 2, section 7, pp. 44–49.

4. Henry Adams, *The Education of Henry Adams,* Boston: Houghton Mifflin Co., 1918, pp. 264–65.

5. See *Nicomachean Ethics,* Book X, Ch. 9, 1179b 1–3.

6. *Nicomachean Ethics* (Thomson translation), Book II, Ch. 4, 1105a 25–b 29.

5. FAILURE AND UNHAPPINESS: ARE THEY OUR OWN RESPONSIBILITY?

1. *The Dialogues of Plato,* trans. by Benjamin Jowett, Oxford: Oxford University Press, 3rd ed., 1892, Vol. II, *Apology,* pp. 125–26 (32 A–D).

2. C. V. Wedgwood, *The King's War,* New York: Macmillan Co., 1959, pp. 79–80.

3. Plato, *Apology,* p. 109 (17 D).

4. Quoted from Joseph Wood Krutch, *Samuel Johnson,* New York: Henry Holt and Co., 1944, pp. 332–33.

5. In what follows we shall no doubt appear to be playing fast and loose both with Plato and with Plato's reputation. It is true that in the dialogue *Protagoras* Plato represents Socrates as advocating a thesis to the effect that virtue is simply

a matter of knowledge and vice of ignorance. However, that this is Plato's own considered view, or that Plato would himself have accepted all of the implications and consequences that we sought to draw out of such a view—neither of these contentions is warranted by the somewhat condensed discussion in the *Protagoras*. Nevertheless, needing to have a convenient label to attach to the sort of ethical position for which Socrates appears to be at least a temporary advocate, we have labeled both the view itself, together with the implications that we have tended to find in it, "Platonic." If such a procedure demands an apology, we willingly offer it—to Plato.

6. BAD LUCK AND THE FORCE OF CIRCUMSTANCES AS CAUSES OF FAILURE

1. Bertrand Russell, *The Analysis of Mind,* London and New York: Macmillan Co., 1921, pp. 61–63.

2. Quoted in Paul Elmer More, *The Sceptical Approach to Religion,* Princeton, N.J.: Princeton University Press, 1934, p. 27.

3. Jerome Hall, *General Principles of Criminal Law,* Indianapolis: Bobbs-Merrill Co., 1947, pp. 386–87.

4. *Ibid.,* pp. 391–92.

5. Aristotle, *Nicomachean Ethics* (Loeb Library translation), Book I, Ch. 9, 1100a 4–9.

6. *Ibid.,* Book I, Ch. 10, 1100b 23–1101a 8.

7. *The Book of Common Prayer,* Psalm 18.

7. BUT WHAT IF GOD IS DEAD?

1. Friedrich Nietzsche, *Der Wille zur Macht,* 55. This is more a paraphrase than a translation.

2. John Stuart Mill, *Utilitarianism,* New York: Liberal Arts Press, 2nd ed., 1957, pp. 44–45.

3. G. E. Moore, *Principia Ethica,* Cambridge: Cambridge University Press, 1st ed., 1903, Ch. III, especially pp. 101–5.

4. Whether it was the existence of these notions that originally accounted for the spread of utilitarianism, or whether it was utilitarianism which caused such notions to be so prevalent, we would not venture to say.

5. See above, Ch. 1.

6. See above, p. 11.

7. Aldous Huxley, *Brave New World,* New York and London: Harper and Brothers, 1946, pp. 263–64.

8. Mill, *Utilitarianism,* p. 14.

9. Moore, *Principia Ethica, passim,* especially Ch. I.

10. Cf. above, Ch. 2, p. 28.

11. If one wished to be pedantic, one might insist that for Aristotle "good" does not belong exclusively to any one category and hence is not susceptible of

definition in the usual sense. However, there is little point in pressing this consideration here.

12. On the fallacy of attempting to pass from statements as to what is or is not the case to statements as to what ought or ought not to be the case, the *locus classicus* is, of course, Hume's *Treatise,* Book III, Part I, section 1. The relevant passage is quoted entire in P. H. Nowell-Smith, *Ethics,* London: Penguin Books, 1954, pp. 36–37.

13. Cf. the well-known article by W. K. Frankena, entitled "The Naturalistic Fallacy," *Mind,* Vol. XLVIII, N. S., No. 192, pp. 465–77.

8. EXISTENTIALISM AND THE CLAIMS OF IRRATIONAL MAN

1. William Barrett, *Irrational Man,* Garden City, N.Y.: Doubleday Anchor Books, 1958, pp. 21–22.

2. *Ibid.,* pp. 45–46.

3. Jean-Paul Sartre, "Existentialism Is a Humanism," in *Existentialism from Dostoyevsky to Sartre,* ed. by Walter Kaufman, New York: Meridian Books, 1958, pp. 294–95.

4. *Kierkegaard's Concluding Unscientific Postscript,* trans. by David F. Swenson and Walter Lowrie, Princeton, N.J.: Princeton University Press, 1944, pp. 118–19.

5. *Ibid.,* p. 280.

6. *Ibid.,* p. 305.

7. *Ibid.,* p. 281.

8. Robert Champigny, *Stages on Sartre's Way,* Bloomington: Indiana University Press, 1959, p. 5.

9. *Kierkegaard's Concluding Unscientific Postscript,* p. 380.

10. Clarence Leuba, *The Natural Man,* Garden City, N.Y.: Doubleday and Co., 1954.

11. To satisfy the requirements of pedantry it should perhaps be noted that such an insistence upon distinguishing the natural from the artificial is characteristically Aristotelian. Cf. Aristotle, *The Physics,* Book II, Ch. 1, 192b 8–32. At the same time, Aristotle would not apply this distinction to the sphere of human moral action in quite the way that Professor Leuba seems to be suggesting it be done.

12. Cf. Aristotle, *The Politics,* Book I, Ch. 8, 1253a 3.

Analytical Table of Contents

Index